WAR FOR DOMINION

Vol. II

DAN LUDDEKE SR.

WAR FOR DOMINION

Vol. II

PUT ON THE ARMOR OF LIGHT

TATE PUBLISHING
AND ENTERPRISES, LLC

Published by Tate Publishing & Enterprises, LLC
127 E. Trade Center Terrace | Mustang, Oklahoma 73064 USA
1.888.361.9473 | www.tatepublishing.com

Tate Publishing is committed to excellence in the publishing industry. The company reflects the philosophy established by the founders, based on Psalm 68:11,
"The Lord gave the word and great was the company of those who published it."

Book design copyright © 2013 by Tate Publishing, LLC. All rights reserved.
Cover design by Rtor Maghuyop
Interior design by Jomar Ouano

Published in the United States of America

ISBN: 978-1-62854-345-2
1. Religion / General
2. Religion / Biblical Studies / General
13.10.29

DEDICATION

This book is dedicated to Jesus of Nazareth, the Holy Son of God who came in the flesh. My Jesus is eternal God who spoke all the creation into existence by His omnipotent Word. My Jesus upholds all the creation in existence by the same omnipotent Word He used to create it. My Jesus is abounding in love and compassion so that He gave Himself as a spotless Lamb to pay for all my sins. My Jesus is holy and righteous and just so that He will wage war against all those who oppose Him, and He will decisively defeat them all. My Jesus is the best thing that ever happened to me. There is nobody better than My Jesus. All praise and glory and power and eternal dominion and authority and majesty to my Jesus, the Christ. I love You, my Lord.

CONTENTS

PREFACE

Every human being, man and woman and child, has an eternal destiny. This is true whether they are believers or unbelievers. The goal and desire of this book is to show from the eternal Word of God how prophecy should encourage and exhort every person who has received the gift of eternal life through faith in the death and resurrection of Jesus Christ to live in a manner worthy of that wondrous salvation. It is evident from the Apostle Peter that this is one of the primary purposes that God gives prophecy.

> But the day of the Lord will come like a thief, in which the heavens will pass away with a roar and the elements will be destroyed with intense heat, and the earth and its works will be burned up. Since all these things are to be destroyed in this way, what sort of people ought you to be in holy conduct and godliness, looking for and hastening the coming of the day of God, because of which the heavens will be destroyed by burning, and the elements will melt with intense heat!
>
> 2 Peter 3:10–12 (NASB)

The universe seems very ancient to humans, but the existence of the current universe is only brief compared to the eternal creation that is yet to come. Peter asks a very logical question in light of this prophetic truth, "What sort of people ought you to be in holy conduct and godliness?" Prophecy enables us to see the big picture of God's plan so we can plan ahead. In light of this prophetic event, it is obviously frivolous and vain for anyone to focus all their efforts in this beginning stage of their existence into the pursuit of things of this present earth.

Volume 1 of this book shows from the Scriptures the important place that God has ordained for the human race in this current yet temporal phase of His creation. Volume 2 continues to examine the place humans have in God's creation plan, with a focus on how this all culminates for Christians in the eternal creation that is yet to come. From the moment of physical birth, every human is thrust into the midst of the war for dominion. Satan has endeavored with all his power to establish his dominion on this one small planet in God's creation, but God has continually thwarted his every effort. God has continually used the weak and frail beings made from the dust of this planet to frustrate Satan's plans to raise himself up to be God's equal. Satan hates the human race. In particular, he hates the humans who have the gift of eternal life through faith in the death and resurrection of Jesus Christ and as a result have been freely given the indwelling Holy Spirit. Every believer's engagement in the war for dominion necessarily involves a continuous battle against their own flesh nature.

> The night is almost gone, and the day is near. Therefore let us lay aside the deeds of darkness and put on the armor of light. Let us behave properly as in the day, not in carousing and drunkenness, not in sexual promiscuity and sensuality, not in strife and jealousy. But put on the Lord Jesus Christ, and make no provision for the flesh in regard to its lusts.
>
> Romans 13:12–14 (NASB)

No human can battle their own flesh nature in their own strength. The flesh nature is too powerful. Believers must continuously rely on the omnipotent Holy Spirit to have the daily ongoing victory. When believers "make no provision for flesh," then the armor of light begins to radiate into the kingdom of darkness currently present on this earth. When believers are arrayed in the armor of light, they manifest the very character and person of Jesus Christ. God can use such believers to thwart Satan's efforts to establish his dominion. Such believers are manifesting the glory of Jesus Christ and will eternally share in His glory.

Every human life on earth is "the grass that withers" during this temporal phase of God's creation.

> For, "ALL FLESH IS LIKE GRASS, AND ALL ITS GLORY LIKE THE FLOWER OF GRASS. THE GRASS WITHERS, AND THE FLOWER FALLS OFF, BUT THE WORD OF THE LORD ENDURES FOREVER." And this is the word which was preached to you.
>
> 1 Peter 1:24–25 (NASB)

Life in this temporal realm is only the beginning of every person's existence. The beginning state of existence of every human is being poured out by God's design. Since every human's temporal life is being poured out and nothing can reverse that, believers might as well make sure they are being poured out as a living sacrifice to God. It is our rightful duty to our Creator and Savior, and it is a very wise plan in preparing of the eternal future. None of us will ever have this blessed opportunity again. By the power of the indwelling Holy Spirit, every believer can begin living their eternal life from the point of salvation. The eternal peace will come as God has foretold, when we will no longer have need for the armor of light. But presently we each live in the midst of a battle, internally and externally.

DOMINION OF MESSIAH

God the Father has already given all authority to Jesus Christ after the resurrection, Matthew 28:18. But Jesus Christ has not yet begun to exercise His full authority. The point at which He begins to fully apply His power is when He opens the seven seals of the scroll given to him by God the Father.

> And He came, and He took it out of the right hand of Him who sat on the throne. And every created thing which is in heaven and on the earth and under the earth and on the sea, and all things in them, I heard saying, "To Him who sits on the throne, and to the Lamb, be blessing and honor and glory and dominion forever and ever."
>
> Revelation 5:7 and 13 (NASB)

With the opening of the seventh seal, the angels with the seven trumpet plagues are sent forth.

> And when He broke the seventh seal, there was silence in heaven for about half an hour. And I saw the seven angels who stand before God; and seven trumpets were given to them.
>
> Revelation 8:1–2 (NASB)

The first act of Jesus Christ in the use of His full authority will be to send forth the seven trumpet plagues on the earth. At the seventh trumpet plague, the heavenly host praises God because the full reign of Jesus Christ has begun.

> And the seventh angel sounded; and there arose loud voices in heaven, saying, "The kingdom of the world has become the kingdom of our Lord, and of His Christ; and He will reign forever and ever." And the twenty-four elders, who sit on their thrones before God, fell on their faces and worshiped God, saying, "We give Thee thanks, O Lord God, the Almighty, who art and who wast, because Thou hast taken Thy great power and hast begun to reign."
>
> Revelation 11:15–17 (NASB)

The kingdom of Jesus Christ is also the kingdom of the Father. When Jesus was on the earth at His first coming, He kept telling the Jews and His disciples that He is One with the Father: John 10:30 and 38, John 14:9–11, John 17:11 and 21. God the Father is the One who establishes the kingdom and total dominion of Christ.

> The Lord says to my Lord: "Sit at My right hand, until I make Thine enemies a footstool for Thy feet."
>
> Psalm 110:1 (NASB)

Jesus Christ, being God, is omnipotent and He has no need for God the Father to make His enemies to be His footstool. Jesus Christ is certainly capable of doing that Himself. But the Father desires to do this for His beloved Son because of what the Son has done for the Father.

> And now says the Lord, who formed Me from the womb to be His Servant, to bring Jacob back to Him, in order

that Israel might be gathered to Him (For I am honored in the sight of the Lord, and My God is My strength), He says, "It is too small a thing that You should be My Servant to raise up the tribes of Jacob, and to restore the preserved ones of Israel; I will also make You a light of the nations so that My salvation may reach to the end of the earth."

Isaiah 49:5–6 (NASB)

God the Father is so pleased that Jesus Christ willfully gave Himself to be His Servant. The Father is pleased that Jesus Christ went forth to bring the beloved people of the Father back to Him. As a reward, the Father will also give Jesus Christ the nations to the ends of the earth. In order for Jesus Christ to be the light of the nations, the nations must be brought into submission to Him. Jesus Christ is now waiting for the Father to accomplish this. He performed all in exact obedience to the will of the Father, John 17:4. But the Son's submission to the will of the Father has not stopped. When Jesus returned to the heavenly holy of holies, the Father told Him to sit at His right hand. Jesus Christ has continually been in His place at the right hand of the Father in obedience through all the time of the church. He will arise and take up the full authority given to Him when the Father says it is time.

Heaven and earth will pass away, but My words shall not pass away. But of that day and hour no one knows, not even the angels of heaven, nor the Son, but the Father alone.

Matthew 24:35–36 (NASB)

The continued submission of the Son to the will of the Father does not in any way diminish the Son's deity. His obedience causes the Father to magnify the glory of the Son all the more. It is an awesome display of the infinite love that exists between the Father, Son, and Holy Spirit. Satan seeks to establish complete dominion out of self-centered, self-promoting arrogance. What Satan seeks to gain by selfishness, Jesus Christ will gain through the humble submission of love. Jesus Christ could easily take the kingdoms of the earth for Himself at any time He chooses apart from the will of the Father. The fact that He doesn't is manifestation of the eternal glory of the godhead. He continues to sit at the right hand of the Father being an Advocate and Intercessor for His body, the church, Romans 8:34 and 1 John 2:1. More will be said about the relationship between the Father and the Son in the chapter "Dominion of All in All."

The day will come when Jesus Christ will leave the place at the right hand of the Father to travel to the earth and be seated in the holy of holies in the temple on the ancient Holy Mountain of God on the earth. When this happens, the Lord will make drastic geographical changes to Mt. Zion and the Holy Land. The Holy Mountain will be elevated in height above all other mountains, and the land around it will be made into a plain.

> All the land will be changed into a plain from Geba to Rimmon south of Jerusalem; but Jerusalem will rise and remain on its site from Benjamin's Gate as far as the place of the First Gate to the Corner Gate, and from the Tower of Hananel to the king's wine presses.
>
> Zechariah 14:10 (NASB)

> Now it will come about that in the last days, the mountain of the house of the Lord will be established as the chief of the mountains, and will be raised above the hills; and all the nations will stream to it.
>
> Isaiah 2:2 (NASB)

The voice of the Lord breaks the cedars; Yes, the Lord breaks in pieces the cedars of Lebanon. And He makes Lebanon skip like a calf, and Sirion like a young wild ox.

Psalm 29:5–6 (NASB)

The area around Mt. Zion will be made into a plain. The Lord Jesus Christ will accomplish this with the command of His voice. It will appear as though the land masses are made to skip. Mt. Zion will be the chief of mountains because it will be the seat of world government, but also it will be physically elevated above all other mountains. It is likely that the Holy Mountain was physically higher than all the other mountains in its original created state. Jerusalem is at the top of Mt. Zion, yet it is in a valley with ridges rising up around it. God must have broken off the upper portion of the mountain when the creation became corrupted by the rebellion. God removed it so Satan could not set up his place on the pinnacle where the throne of God once resided. God refers to this past action as an analogy of what He will do to Satan.

"Behold, I am against you, O destroying mountain, who destroys the whole earth," declares the Lord, "And I will stretch out My hand against you, and roll you down from the crags and I will make you a burnt out mountain."

Jeremiah 51:25 (NASB)

Satan's attempts to rule the earth always result in destruction on the earth. He has delusions that he will rule from the top of a mountain of splendor as Mt. Zion once was. But as the splendor of Mt. Zion was removed when it was broken off, so also the splendor of Lucifer was removed when he was cast from the Holy Mountain. God says Satan will not be a mountain of splendor but a burned out mountain.

In the promised kingdom age, the Holy Mountain will be restored to the splendor it had before the angelic rebellion. The remnant of Israel left on the earth after the great tribulation will be gathered to the renewed Mt. Zion. There the Lord will wash and cleanse them of their sins.

> In that day the Branch of the Lord will be beautiful and glorious, and the fruit of the earth will be the pride and the adornment of the survivors of Israel. And it will come about that he who is left in Zion and remains in Jerusalem will be called holy—everyone who is recorded for life in Jerusalem. When the Lord has washed away the filth of the daughters of Zion, and purged the bloodshed of Jerusalem from her midst, by the spirit of judgment and the spirit of burning, then the Lord will create over the whole area of Mount Zion and over her assemblies a cloud by day, even smoke, and the brightness of a flaming fire by night; for over all the glory will be a canopy. And there will be a shelter to give shade from the heat by day, and refuge and protection from the storm and the rain.
>
> Isaiah 4:2–6 (NASB)

The Shechinah glory cloud that was over the tabernacle and led Israel in the wilderness will be over all of the Holy Mountain in the kingdom age. Imagine approaching Mt. Zion and seeing the towering mountain with the canopy of God covering it, a pillar of cloud by day and of fire by night. The origin of the cloud will be the temple where Jesus Christ is seated as the absolute sovereign over the whole earth.

Not only will the ancient Holy Mountain be renovated, but the Holy Land will also be drastically changed back to being like Eden, the garden of God.

> The Lord will surely comfort Zion and will look with compassion on all her ruins; he will make her deserts like

Eden, her wastelands like the garden of the LORD. Joy and gladness will be found in her, thanksgiving and the sound of singing.

Isaiah 51:3 (NASB)

'This is what the Sovereign LORD says: On the day I cleanse you from all your sins, I will resettle your towns, and the ruins will be rebuilt. The desolate land will be cultivated instead of lying desolate in the sight of all who pass through it. They will say, "This land that was laid waste has become like the garden of Eden; the cities that were lying in ruins, desolate and destroyed, are now fortified and inhabited." Then the nations around you that remain will know that I the LORD have rebuilt what was destroyed and have replanted what was desolate. I the Lord have spoken, and I will do it.

Ezekiel 36:33–36 (NASB)

Much of the land promised to Abraham is not useful for cultivation. When the Lord refurbishes the Holy Land, it will be a plush vegetated garden. There will be rivers flowing from the temple, one going west to the Mediterranean Sea and one going east to the north end of the Dead Sea. All the desert area north of the Dead Sea will become a plush garden. The Dead Sea will be made into a body of fresh water.

And in that day living waters will flow out of Jerusalem, half of them toward the eastern sea and the other half toward the western sea; it will be in summer as well as in winter.

Zechariah 14:8 (NASB)

Then he brought me back to the door of the house; and behold, water was flowing from under the threshold of the house toward the east, for the house faced east. And the water was flowing down from under, from the right side of the house, from south of the altar.

Ezekiel 47:1 (NASB)

Then he said to me, "These waters go out toward the eastern region and go down into the Arabah; then they go toward the sea, being made to flow into the sea, and the waters of the sea become fresh."

Ezekiel 47:8 (NASB)

And by the river on its bank, on one side and on the other, will grow all kinds of trees for food. Their leaves will not wither, and their fruit will not fail. They will bear every month because their water flows from the sanctuary, and their fruit will be for food and their leaves for healing.

Ezekiel 47:12 (NASB)

The wilderness and the desert will be glad, and the Arabah will rejoice and blossom; like the crocus it will blossom profusely and rejoice with rejoicing and shout of joy. The glory of Lebanon will be given to it, the majesty of Carmel and Sharon.

Isaiah 35:1–2 (NASB)

And it will come about in that day that the mountains will drip with sweet wine, and the hills will flow with milk, and all the brooks of Judah will flow with water; and a spring will go out from the house of the Lord, to water the valley of Shittim.

Joel 3:18 (NASB)

These miraculous geographical changes are promised for the ancient Holy Land only. No prophecy is given about such miraculous renovations anywhere else on the earth. The promised land will be like heaven on earth. The kingdom age is an intermediate step between the eternal estate and the current fallen state of the earth. In the kingdom age, the creation as a whole will continue to groan having been subjected to futility by the Creator.

> For the anxious longing of the creation waits eagerly for the revealing of the sons of God. For the creation was subjected to futility, not of its own will, but because of Him who subjected it, in hope that the creation itself also will be set free from its slavery to corruption into the freedom of the glory of the children of God. For we know that the whole creation groans and suffers the pains of childbirth together until now.
>
> Romans 8:19–22 (NASB)

There will still be sinful humans living on the earth during the thousand-year kingdom age of Jesus Messiah. That is why Jesus will have to rule the nations with a rod of iron, Psalm 2. The groans and the suffering of the "whole creation" will continue as long as the groans, and suffering of the human race continues. The whole creation is referring to the earth and all the stellar space. It won't be until all the "sons of God" from all human history are revealed in glory that the whole creation "will be set free from its slavery and corruption." The "setting free" refers to the renovation of the whole earth and all the heavens to make the new heaven and the new earth of the eternal estate, Revelation 21:1. But in the thousand-year kingdom age, only the land promised to Abraham, Isaac, and Jacob will be transformed. The reason is that Messiah wants to make the promised land the most desirable place on the earth to draw the people of all nations to Him. God placed the first human in the paradise called Eden, and humans have desired to be in paradise and a place of rest ever since. The modern-day theme parks are evidence of this with the rides, animal exhibits, flowing clear waters, exquisite food, and luxurious living quarters.

The attraction of the promised land in the kingdom age will far exceed anything man-made theme parks offer as far as being a paradise. The animal exhibit will be unprecedented.

> And the wolf will dwell with the lamb, and the leopard will lie down with the kid, and the calf and the young lion and the fatling together; and a little boy will lead them. Also the cow and the bear will graze; their young will lie down together; and the lion will eat straw like the ox. And the nursing child will play by the hole of the cobra, and the weaned child will put his hand on the viper's den. They will not hurt or destroy in all My holy mountain, for the earth will be full of the knowledge of the Lord as the waters cover the sea.
>
> Isaiah 11:6–9 (NASB)

In the Holy Land and on Mt. Zion, the animal kingdom will revert to being as it was in the garden of Eden with Adam and Eve. Prophecy does not indicate this change in the animal kingdom will take place anywhere else but the ancient Holy Mountain of God. Most likely this transformation will be for all the Holy Land to complement the geographical changes.

> Behold, I will do something new, now it will spring forth; will you not be aware of it? I will even make a roadway in the wilderness, rivers in the desert. The beasts of the field will glorify Me; the jackals and the ostriches; because I have given waters in the wilderness and rivers in the desert, to give drink to My chosen people.
>
> Isaiah 43:19–20 (NASB)

The promised land will again truly be made into Eden, the garden of God, a paradise of praise and glory to the Creator and Sustainer of all that exists. The promised land will be the place to enjoy both the creation and the physical presence of the Creator. There will be no idolatry of trying to find fulfillment in the creation apart from the Creator. As covered in the chapter "The Woman and the Scarlet Beast" in volume 1, Satan will have turned Mt. Zion and the Holy Land into a most unholy place full of all forms of idolatry and depraved entertainment that the fallen human race has craved for fulfillment. This will be Satan's counterfeit of the true fulfillment that the human race will experience in the beautiful land when Jesus Christ miraculously transforms Mt. Zion and the Holy Land back to being like Eden. It will truly be the place to take the whole family.

In the eternal estate, the walls around the New Jerusalem will be made of jasper, with gates made of single pearls and foundation stone adorned with precious jewels, Revelation 21:10–21. So also the walls around Jerusalem in the kingdom age will be made with precious and costly materials.

> O afflicted one, storm-tossed, and not comforted, behold, I will set your stones in antimony, and your foundations I will lay in sapphires. Moreover, I will make your battlements of rubies, and your gates of crystal, and your entire wall of precious stones.
>
> Isaiah 54:11–12 (NASB)

It can be known that this is not prophecy about the New Jerusalem because of the differences in the descriptions. There are walls made of precious stone compared to walls made of jasper. There are gates of crystal compared to gates of single pearls. There are foundation stones of sapphires compared to foundation stones adorned with every precious stone. The costly materials used for the walls of Jerusalem in the kingdom age tells of the great wealth Israel will possess.

And your gates will be open continually; they will not be closed day or night, so that men may bring to you the wealth of the nations, with their kings led in procession.

Isaiah 60:11 (NASB)

You will also suck the milk of nations, and will suck the breast of kings; then you will know that I, the Lord, am your Savior, and your Redeemer, the Mighty One of Jacob.

Isaiah 60:16 (NASB)

Israel was so wealthy in the days of Solomon that silver was considered common.

And all King Solomon's drinking vessels were of gold, and all the vessels of the house of the forest of Lebanon were of pure gold. None was of silver; it was not considered valuable in the days of Solomon.

1 Kings 10:21 (NASB)

In the kingdom age, not only will silver be considered common, but precious stones will also. Taking it one step further into the eternal estate, not only will silver and precious stones be common, but pure gold will also be common as it will be used to pave the streets, Revelation 21:21. Israel is going to be a very blessed people in the thousand-year kingdom of Christ. The nations of the earth that walk in obedience to Jesus Christ will also be blessed, but God's chosen people will be the most prosperous.

In addition to the geographical changes at the beginning of the kingdom age, all the believers, Jew and gentile, who have survived the great tribulation will be miraculously healed and made whole for entrance into the kingdom of Jesus Christ.

Then the eyes of the blind will be opened, and the ears of the deaf will be unstopped. Then the lame will leap like a deer, and the tongue of the dumb will shout for joy. For waters will break forth in the wilderness and streams in the Arabah. And the scorched land will become a pool, and the thirsty ground springs of water; in the haunt of jackals, its resting place, grass becomes reeds and rushes.

Isaiah 35:5–7 (NASB)

There was a partial fulfillment of this prophecy at the first coming of Jesus Christ. It was meant as a sign to the Jews that He was the Messiah. In addition to healing, people in the kingdom age are going to once again live for hundreds of years as people did before the flood.

For behold, I create new heavens and a new earth; and the former things shall not be remembered or come to mind. But be glad and rejoice forever in what I create; for behold, I create Jerusalem for rejoicing, and her people for gladness. I will also rejoice in Jerusalem, and be glad in My people; and there will no longer be heard in her the voice of weeping and the sound of crying. No longer will there be in it an infant who lives but a few days, or an old man who does not live out his days; for the youth will die at the age of one hundred and the one who does not reach the age of one hundred shall be thought accursed.

Isaiah 65:17–20 (NASB)

Part of this prophecy is about the thousand-year kingdom age, and part of it is about the eternal estate. The Old Testament prophecies did not distinguish between the thousand-year messianic kingdom and the eternal estate. In both the kingdom age and the eternal estate, Jerusalem will be created for rejoicing. But in the messianic kingdom, there will not be a new heavens and new earth. Those come after the thousand-year kingdom. However, in the eternal estate, there will be no more physical death, Revelation 21:4. The first part of this prophecy is about the eternal estate with the new heavens and new earth and the New Jerusalem. The latter part of this prophecy is about the kingdom age with the renovated Jerusalem where there will still be physical death. When Jesus Christ reigns upon this earth, physical death will still be a reality, but peoples' life spans will be greatly increased.

All the people of the gentile nations left alive on the earth will go through a judgment before the Lord Jesus Christ.

> But when the Son of Man comes in His glory, and all the angels with Him, then He will sit on His glorious throne. And all the nations will be gathered before Him; and He will separate them from one another, as the shepherd separates the sheep from the goats; and He will put the sheep on His right, and the goats on the left.
>
> Matthew 25:31–33 (NASB)

The sheep are believers, and the goats are unbelievers. The separation is based on whether they have been saved by faith. After separation, the works of each individual in each group will be evaluated by Jesus Christ. The works of the gentile believers left alive on the earth are evaluated to determine reward.

> Then the King will say to those on His right, "Come, you who are blessed of My Father, inherit the kingdom prepared for you from the foundation of the world. For I was hungry, and you gave Me something to eat; I was thirsty, and you gave Me drink; I was a stranger, and you invited Me in; naked, and you clothed Me; I was sick, and you visited Me; I was in prison, and you came to Me." Then the righteous will answer Him, saying, "Lord, when did we see You hungry, and feed You, or thirsty, and give You drink? And when did we see You a stranger, and invite You in, or naked, and clothe You? And when did we see

You sick, or in prison, and come to You?" And the King will answer and say to them, "Truly I say to you, to the extent that you did it to one of these brothers of Mine, even the least of them, you did it to Me."

Matthew 25:34–40 (NASB)

"These brothers of Mine" refers to Israel in the great tribulation period. Gentiles who befriend the people of Israel in their midst will be recognized and will be rewarded by Jesus Christ at the start of the kingdom age. Gentile believers who mistreated the Jews by not giving them a drink or food or clothing will be made slaves of Israel as their punishment.

And the peoples will take them along and bring them to their place, and the house of Israel will possess them as an inheritance in the land of the Lord as male servants and female servants; and they will take their captors captive, and will rule over their oppressors.

Isaiah 14:2 (NASB)

"Then they shall bring all your brethren from all the nations as a grain offering to the Lord, on horses, in chariots, in litters, on mules, and on camels, to My holy mountain Jerusalem," says the Lord, "just as the sons of Israel bring their grain offering in a clean vessel to the house of the Lord."

Isaiah 66:20 (NASB)

Israel will be gathered from all the nations into the renovated promised land to enjoy the blessing of Messiah. The gentiles left on the earth will transport them there. In the great tribulation period, the Jews will be greatly persecuted by the people of the nations where they are exiled. The gentiles will bring them to the Lord at Mt. Zion in fear and trembling having seen the annihilation He brought upon His enemies. The Jews brought to the Lord by these gentiles will be as a peace offering in hopes that He will not bring His wrath upon them because of their mistreatment of His treasured ones. Those gentiles will be made captives and servants to the people of Israel. Although this will serve as punishment, it will also be a blessing because they will be in the promised land made to be like Eden, in close proximity to the Messiah.

The works of the gentile unbelievers left alive on the earth will also be evaluated according to the standard of the great white throne judgment, Revelation 20:11–15. The purpose of this judgment is to determine if they have adequate righteousness to enter the kingdom. They will be found to be woefully short of God's righteous standard.

> Then He will also say to those on His left, "Depart from Me, accursed ones, into the eternal fire which has been prepared for the devil and his angels; for I was hungry, and you gave Me nothing to eat; I was thirsty, and you gave Me nothing to drink; I was a stranger, and you did not invite Me in; naked, and you did not clothe Me; sick, and in prison, and you did not visit Me." Then they themselves also will answer, saying, "Lord, when did we see You hungry, or thirsty, or a stranger, or naked, or sick, or in prison, and did not take care of You?" Then He will answer them, saying, "Truly I say to you, to the extent that you did not do it to one of the least of these, you did not do it to Me." And these will go away into eternal punishment, but the righteous into eternal life.
>
> Matthew 25:41–46 (NASB)

They will be immediately cast into the eternal lake of fire along with the beast and the false prophet.

After all unbelievers are removed from the earth, there will be a universal outpouring of the Holy Spirit on all the inhabitants of the earth.

> And it will come about after this that I will pour out My Spirit on all mankind; and your sons and daughters will prophesy, your old men will dream dreams, your young men will see visions. And even on the male and female servants I will pour out My Spirit in those days.
>
> Joel 2:28–29 (NASB)

God will not give His Holy Spirit to unbelievers, so all the inhabitants on the earth at the start of the reign of Jesus Christ will be believers. Unlike the world now, knowledge of God will be commonplace among the peoples of the earth.

> "And they shall not teach again, each man his neighbor and each man his brother, saying, 'Know the Lord,' for they shall all know Me, from the least of them to the greatest of them," declares the Lord, "for I will forgive their iniquity, and their sin I will remember no more."
>
> Jeremiah 31:34 (NASB)

It is the giving of the Holy Spirit that will enable all the peoples of the earth to know the Lord. This is true today in the church for believers who continually walk in the Spirit, 1 John 2:27.

When Jesus Christ has dominion on the earth, the nations will no longer know war. They will go to the Holy Mountain seeking His wise council, and He will judge between the nations.

> Now it will come about that in the last days, the mountain of the house of the Lord will be established as the chief of the mountains, and will be raised above the hills; and all the nations will stream to it. And many peoples will come and say, "Come, let us go up to the mountain of the Lord,

to the house of the God of Jacob; that He may teach us concerning His ways, and that we may walk in His paths." For the law will go forth from Zion, and the word of the Lord from Jerusalem. And He will judge between the nations, and will render decisions for many peoples; and they will hammer their swords into plowshares, and their spears into pruning hooks. Nation will not lift up sword against nation, and never again will they learn war.

Isaiah 2:2–4 (NASB)

Satan has continually used war and violence in an attempt to overcome the barriers God has placed on the human race to protect it. The languages and races of the peoples will not be an obstacle to Jesus Christ when He rules over the nations. He will have no need to make everyone speak the same language. The nations will understand His authority as He will rule them with a rod of iron, Psalm 2:7–12. Jesus Christ will withhold His blessing from those nations that refuse to go up to Him on His Holy Mountain.

Then it will come about that any who are left of all the nations that went against Jerusalem will go up from year to year to worship the King, the Lord of hosts, and to celebrate the Feast of Booths. And it will be that whichever of the families of the earth does not go up to Jerusalem to worship the King, the Lord of hosts, there will be no rain on them. And if the family of Egypt does not go up or enter, then no rain will fall on them; it will be the plague with which the Lord smites the nations who do not go up to celebrate the Feast of Booths. This will be the punishment of Egypt, and the punishment of all the nations who do not go up to celebrate the Feast of Booths.

Zechariah 14:16–19 (NASB)

Behold, the nations are like a drop from a bucket, and are regarded as a speck of dust on the scales; behold, He lifts up the islands like fine dust. All the nations are as nothing

before Him, they are regarded by Him as less than nothing
and meaningless.

Isaiah 40:15 and 17 (NASB)

The believers left alive on the earth will enter the kingdom with
their flesh natures intact, and they will be prone to sin, even with
Satan removed. Jesus Christ intends that all the people of the
earth be blessed by Israel and His glorious presence in the midst
of His people. The nations of the world who walk in the light of
Jesus Christ will be richly blessed and prosperous. Most of the
inhabitants of the earth will diligently look for any opportunity
to go to Mt. Zion to see the Lord.

> Thus says the Lord of hosts, "It will yet be that peoples
> will come, even the inhabitants of many cities. And the
> inhabitants of one will go to another saying, Let us go
> at once to entreat the favor of the Lord, and to seek the
> Lord of hosts; I will also go. So many peoples and mighty
> nations will come to seek the Lord of hosts in Jerusalem
> and to entreat the favor of the Lord." Thus says the Lord
> of hosts, "In those days ten men from all the nations will
> grasp the garment of a Jew saying, 'Let us go with you, for
> we have heard that God is with you.'"
>
> Zechariah 8:20–23 (NASB)

When Jews travel internationally, people will ask them if they
can return to the Holy Land with them to be in the presence of
the Lord.

Ezekiel 40–48 describes the temple and Mount Zion in the
kingdom age. When the temple is completed, the Lord Jesus
Christ will take His rightful place in the Holy of Holies.

> Then he led me to the gate, the gate facing toward the
> east; and behold, the glory of the God of Israel was coming

from the way of the east. And His voice was like the sound of many waters; and the earth shone with His glory.

Ezekiel 43:1–2 (NASB)

And the glory of the Lord came into the house by the way of the gate facing toward the east. And the Spirit lifted me up and brought me into the inner court; and behold, the glory of the Lord filled the house.

Ezekiel 43:4–5 (NASB)

The outer gate on the east side of the temple where Jesus Christ enters will be locked and never opened. Nobody will be allowed to enter through that gate. However, David will be allowed to enter through the side door of the east gate. David will be raised up and made prince over the nation Israel.

Then I will set over them one shepherd, My servant David, and he will feed them; he will feed them himself and be their shepherd. And I, the Lord, will be their God, and My servant David will be prince among them; I, the Lord, have spoken.

Ezekiel 34:23–24 (NASB)

David will share in the dominion of Messiah on the earth. He will be the shepherd and the prince over God's chosen people. David was the king who so desired the presence of the Lord that he brought the ark of God to Jerusalem, dancing before it with great energy. But the presence of the ark was not sufficient. He then wanted to build a house for God in Jerusalem. David wanted God to live next door. Because he so earnestly desired to be in the Lord's presence, the Lord will reward David with an awesome privilege in the kingdom age.

And the Lord said to me, "This gate shall be shut; it shall not be opened, and no one shall enter by it, for the Lord

God of Israel has entered by it; therefore it shall be shut. As for the prince, he shall sit in it as prince to eat bread before the Lord; he shall enter by way of the porch of the gate, and shall go out by the same way."

Ezekiel 44:2–3 (NASB)

And when the prince provides a freewill offering, a burnt offering, or peace offerings *as* a freewill offering to the Lord, the gate facing east shall be opened for him. And he shall provide his burnt offering and his peace offerings as he does on the sabbath day. Then he shall go out, and the gate shall be shut after he goes out.

Ezekiel 46:12 (NASB)

David will also be the only one who will have the honor of being able to go to the temple anytime to offer a sacrifice to the Lord, and the door will be opened for him. There will be designated times when the rest of the people will be able to go before the Lord. Ezekiel 46 describes the procedure for the people going into the temple area and offering sacrifices before the Lord.

Thus says the Lord God, "The gate of the inner court facing east shall be shut the six working days; but it shall be opened on the sabbath day, and opened on the day of the new moon."

Ezekiel 46:1 (NASB)

The people of the land shall also worship at the doorway of that gate before the Lord on the sabbaths and on the new moons.

Ezekiel 46:3 (NASB)

And when the prince enters, he shall go in by way of the porch of the gate and go out by the same way. But when the people of the land come before the Lord at the appointed feasts, he who enters by way of the north gate to worship shall go out by way of the south gate. And he who enters by way of the south gate shall go out by way of the north gate.

Ezekiel 46:8–9 (NASB)

The inner gate of the temple on the east side will be closed except for the Sabbath and the day of the new moon. On those days, the east-side inner court gate of the temple will be open, and the people will be able to see Jesus Christ seated in the temple as they offer their sacrifices. The people will be able to enter and exit the temple area by the outer gates on the south and the north sides. The mandate that people leave through a different gate than the one by which they entered will symbolize the change they will experience in their face-to-face encounter with the Lord Jesus Christ. When they exit, they will not be the same people they were when they entered. Every visit to the temple of Jesus will be a life-changing experience. Even though we are unable to physically see and hear the Lord in this age, we should also be changed in our every encounter with Jesus Christ. Only the prince David will be able to enter and exit the temple area by the side door of the outer gate on the east side to go before the presence of the Lord to bring his sacrifice.

In the inner court, on the east side of the temple, there will be an altar before the Lord, Ezekiel 40:47. A detailed description of the altar is given in Ezekiel 43:13–18. There will be animal sacrifices burned on the altar, Ezekiel 40:38–43, 43:19–27, 44:11, 45:17-25. The sacrifices will be done according to the procedure given in the Mosaic law.

> Speak to the sons of Israel and say to them, "When any man of you brings an offering to the Lord, you shall bring your offering of animals from the herd or the flock. If his offering is a burnt offering from the herd, he shall offer

it, a male without defect; he shall offer it at the doorway of the tent of meeting, that he may be accepted before the Lord. And he shall lay his hand on the head of the burnt offering, that it may be accepted for him to make atonement on his behalf. And he shall slay the young bull before the Lord; and Aaron's sons, the priests, shall offer up the blood and sprinkle the blood around on the altar that is at the doorway of the tent of meeting. He shall then skin the burnt offering and cut it into its pieces. And the sons of Aaron the priest shall put fire on the altar and arrange wood on the fire. Then Aaron's sons, the priests, shall arrange the pieces, the head, and the suet over the wood which is on the fire that is on the altar. Its entrails, however, and its legs he shall wash with water. And the priest shall offer up in smoke all of it on the altar for a burnt offering, an offering by fire of a soothing aroma to the Lord."

Leviticus 1:2–9 (NASB)

It is reasonable to think that there would not be the need for animal sacrifices to the Lord in the kingdom age, since the sacrifice of Jesus Christ was satisfactory to the Father, Hebrews 9:11–14. The people left on the earth in bodies of flesh will still have their sinful natures, so they will fall in sin the same as humans do today. When people of Israel and of the nations go to the temple on Mt. Zion to the presence of the Lamb of God, place their hands on the head of the animal being sacrificed, watch as the animal's throat is cut and the life pours out of it, then watch as the sacrifice is burned, they will be experiencing a dramatic reminder of what the One seated on the throne in radiant glory did for them on the cross. Those who do not go to Mt. Zion to make sacrifices will forget what the Lord has done for them, and they will stray away from Him in their hearts.

Other people who are found worthy will also share in the dominion of Jesus Christ in the thousand-year kingdom. The disciples who walked with Jesus at His first coming will reign over the twelve tribes of Israel, Luke 22:28–30. The martyrs from the time of the great tribulation will reign with Jesus Christ on this earth, Revelation 20:4–6. Believers of the church age who endure in their faith will reign with Jesus Christ, 2 Timothy 2:12 and Revelation 2:26–28. These verses about the church will be examined closer in the chapter "Gathering of the Faithful."

When Jesus Christ displaces Satan as the ruler of this world, many miraculous transformations will take place. It will be like the difference between night and day. Prior to the Lord's return, Satan will also attempt to bring changes to the world when he displays himself as God in the temple on Mt. Zion, but those changes will be destructive. Satan is no God. When Jesus Christ takes His rightful place on Mt. Zion, He will bring change by rejuvenation. For those who survive the great tribulation, the reign of Jesus Christ from the Holy Mountain will be a most refreshing change from the former tyranny.

> Be joyful with Jerusalem and rejoice for her, all you who love her; be exceedingly glad with her, all you who mourn over her, that you may nurse and be satisfied with her comforting breasts, that you may suck and be delighted with her bountiful bosom. For thus says the Lord, "Behold, I extend peace to her like a river, and the glory of the nations like an overflowing stream; and you shall be nursed, you shall be carried on the hip and fondled on the knees. As one whom his mother comforts, so I will comfort you; and you shall be comforted in Jerusalem." Then you shall see this, and your heart shall be glad, and your bones shall flourish like the new grass; and the hand of the Lord shall be made known to His servants. But He shall be indignant toward His enemies.
>
> Isaiah 66:10–14 (NASB)

When Jesus Christ rules the world from Mt. Zion, Jerusalem and Israel will finally be the light to the world that God has long desired them to be.

> You are the light of the world. A city set on a hill cannot be hidden. Nor do men light a lamp, and put it under the peck-measure, but on the lamp stand; and it gives light to all who are in the house. Let your light shine before men in such a way that they may see your good works, and glorify your Father who is in heaven.
>
> Matthew 5:14–16 (NASB)

DOMINION OF ALL IN ALL

Jesus will rule on a partially renovated earth for a thousand years. After the final Satan-led human rebellion on the earth, Satan is immediately cast into the lake of fire. All who still remain in the grave on the earth will be called forth by Jesus Christ. Then He will judge them from His great white throne.

> And I saw a great white throne and Him who sat upon it, from whose presence earth and heaven fled away, and no place was found for them. And I saw the dead, the great and the small, standing before the throne, and books were opened; and another book was opened, which is the book of life; and the dead were judged from the things which were written in the books, according to their deeds.
>
> Revelation 20:11–12 (NASB)

The earth and heaven are moved out of the way for the great white throne of Jesus Christ. The writer of Hebrews quotes Psalm 102 to describe this same event.

> And, "Thou, Lord, in the beginning didst lay the foundation of the earth, and the heavens are the works of Thy hands; they will perish, but Thou remainest; and they all will become old as a garment, and as a mantle Thou

wilt roll them up; as a garment they will also be changed. But Thou art the same, and Thy years will not come to an end."

Hebrews 1:10–12 (NASB)

The Greek word translated *will perish* can also mean to "make void." There are passages of Scripture that say the earth is eternal, meaning it will never be destroyed.

He built his sanctuary like the heights, like the earth that he established forever.

Psalm 78:69 (NASB)

He established the earth upon its foundations, so that it will not totter forever and ever.

Psalm 104:5 (NASB)

Generations come and generations go, but the earth remains forever.

Ecclesiastes 1:4 (NASB)

The Apostle Peter also gives insight as to what will happen to the earth at the end of the thousand-year messianic kingdom.

But the day of the Lord will come like a thief, in which the heavens will pass away with a roar and the elements will be destroyed with intense heat, and the earth and its works will be burned up.

2 Peter 3:10 (NASB)

The new earth will not be a new physical mass. It will be the old earth completely renovated. All that is on the surface of the earth will be made void when Jesus Christ purges and disinfects it with intense heat. All the things that humans idolize on the earth will be incinerated. Before Jesus Christ purges the earth, He will call forth all those who remain in the grave and will remove all living beings off the earth.

> "I will completely remove all things from the face of the earth," declares the Lord. "I will remove man and beast; I will remove the birds of the sky and the fish of the sea, and the ruins along with the wicked; and I will cut off man from the face of the earth," declares the Lord.
>
> Zephaniah 1:2–3 (NASB)

Jesus Christ will do this just before the earth and heaven are rolled up like an old garment to move them out of the way of the great white throne.

After all judgment is completed, Jesus Christ, the Creator of all, will make a new heaven and a new earth out of the old heaven and the old earth.

> And I saw a new heaven and a new earth; for the first heaven and the first earth passed away, and there is no longer any sea.
>
> Revelation 21:1 (NASB)

All creation is going to be restored to its original state. God liked the way it was before the angelic war. The earth originally had no sea. The water that covered the earth came as judgment. There will be no more need for judgment on the new earth, so there will be no sea. The seas have also functioned as barriers dividing the continents and the nations of the peoples. There will no longer be any need for the barriers of the seas between the nations on the new earth. As covered previously in the chapter "The Holy Mountain of God" in volume 1, the new earth will have an eternal Holy Mountain. The new earth will also have a promised land for the descendents of Abraham, Isaac, and Jacob. God promised the land to them as their eternal possession.

> And the Lord said to Abram, after Lot had separated from him, "Now lift up your eyes and look from the place where you are, northward and southward and eastward and westward; for all the land which you see, I will give it to you and to your descendants forever."
>
> Genesis 13:14–15 (NASB)

The new Holy Land will be the land surrounding the new Holy Mountain, which will be for the nation of Israel. The new earth is going to be completely populated with people. Because there will be no sea on the new earth, an additional two-thirds of the earth's surface will be freed up as living space. But the nation of Israel will have the most prominent and desirable place on the new earth around the new Holy Mountain of God.

> And the nations will know that I am the Lord who sanctifies Israel, when My sanctuary is in their midst forever.
>
> Ezekiel 37:28 (NASB)

On the new earth other nations will also still exist. God is not going to remove the racial and national barriers that He established at the Tower of Babel. The fact that there are people from every tribe and language on the new earth is to the glory of God. The enemy was so sure they all belonged to him and that they were his to give to whomever he desired. The nations on the new earth will be an eternal reminder that God alone is sovereign over all. There will be kings over the nations on the new earth.

> And the nations shall walk by its light, and the kings of the earth shall bring their glory into it. And in the daytime

(for there shall be no night there) its gates shall never be closed; and they shall bring the glory and the honor of the nations into it.

Revelation 21:24–26 (NASB)

The glory of the nations on the current fallen earth belongs to the most powerful nations. On the new earth the glory of the nations will be their produce which could include food or manufactured goods. The kings of the nations will bring the produce of their people as an offering to the Lord who is the Giver of the produce to the nations. The gates of the New Jerusalem will never be closed because there will be no sin present on the new earth. This is in contrast to the thousand-year reign of Jesus Christ when there will still be sin present on the earth. The gate of the inner sanctuary of the messianic temple on Mt. Zion will be open only on the Sabbath and on the day of the new moon, Ezekiel 46:1.

In the New Jerusalem, the river of life will flow from the throne of God and the Lamb.

And he showed me a river of the water of life, clear as crystal, coming from the throne of God and of the Lamb, in the middle of its street. And on either side of the river was the tree of life, bearing twelve kinds of fruit, yielding its fruit every month; and the leaves of the tree were for the healing of the nations.

Revelation 22:1–2 (NASB)

In Revelation 5:6, John writes that the Lamb has the appearance "as if slain." This means that Jesus Christ will be in His resurrection body bearing the scars of the crucifixion on His hands and feet and side. This will be an eternal reminder of the extravagant price of the love gift of God that redeemed us. The Holy Spirit will have an eternal physical manifestation at the throne in the New Jerusalem along with God (the Father) and the Lamb (Jesus

Christ). The Holy Spirit is the water of life. John, the writer of Revelation, gives the key to understanding this in the gospel he wrote.

> "He who believes in Me, as the Scripture said, 'From his innermost being shall flow rivers of living water.'" But this He spoke of the Spirit, whom those who believed in Him were to receive; for the Spirit was not yet given, because Jesus was not yet glorified.
>
> John 7:38–39 (NASB)

Growing on either side of the river of life is the tree of life. In the garden of Eden, Adam and Eve ate from the tree of life to sustain their lives, Genesis 3:22. When the new earth comes, the bride of Christ will have already lived in resurrection bodies for a thousand years. There is no mention of their need to eat from the tree of life to sustain their lives during that period. The tree of life will have a different purpose in the New Jerusalem. The leaves are for the healing of the nations. Certainly there will be no more conflict between the nations or racial tensions on the new earth. Humans will no longer be burdened by sinful, fallen flesh natures. Although the violent history of nations devouring nations and acts of ethnic cleansing will be forgiven, there will apparently still be a need for healing between the nations. God could easily make all those in the eternal estate to be one race, but God will retain the national boundaries. It will be an eternal reminder of the goodness the Creator displayed in dividing the human race into the nations to protect humanity from destruction at the hand of Satan. It will be an eternal reminder that only the Creator is able to overcome the boundaries that He establishes in His creation. The leaves of the tree of life will be God's provision that will enable the nations on the new earth to transcend their national boundaries to be able to serve and worship Him in unity forever. The tree of life grows on either side of the river of life. The river of life, which is the Holy

Spirit, waters the tree of life. The Spirit will make the tree of life thrive and be lush with the healing leaves. The fruit growing on the tree of life is the fruit of the Spirit, a different fruit each month. In Galatians 5:22 and 23 Paul gives the traits of the fruit of the Spirit. In this present age, the fruit of the Spirit is the very character of God given to the children of God. In the New Jerusalem, people who have the right to the tree of life will eat its fruit, Revelation 22:14. People will also drink of the water of life, Revelation 21:6. The divine nature, the character of the Holy Spirit, will be imparted to all the people through the leaves of the tree of life, through the eating of the fruit and the drinking of the water of life. The Holy Spirit will enable the nations to live in the unity of divine love and character for all eternity. They will thrive in the same unity of love and character that exists between the Father, Son, and Holy Spirit. As the tree of life thrives and bears fruit continuously, so the nations together will thrive and bear produce continually to bring to the throne of God and the Lamb.

In the New Jerusalem, there will be people permanently present from every nation and language eternally serving God and the Lamb at their throne.

> After these things I looked, and behold, a great multitude, which no one could count, from every nation and all tribes and peoples and tongues, standing before the throne and before the Lamb, clothed in white robes, and palm branches were in their hands;
>
> Revelation 7:9 (NASB)

> These are the ones who come out of the great tribulation, and they have washed their robes and made them white in the blood of the Lamb. For this reason, they are before the throne of God; and they serve Him day and night in His temple; and He who sits on the throne shall spread His tabernacle over them.
>
> Revelation 7:14–15 (NASB)

These people will be the multitude of obedient believers from every race and nation who have been faithful in the great tribulation period, so many that John says they cannot be counted. The great tribulation will be the most difficult time in human history to be faithful to God and to walk in righteousness. In the history of wars between nations, conquering kings have often taken people of royalty captive from the conquered nation. (Biblical examples include Daniel and his three friends, Daniel 1:3–4, and Nehemiah 1:11. In Isaiah 39:7, God gave prophecy to King Hezekiah that this would happen to the royalty of Judah.) The royal captives were made to serve as slaves in the palace of the conquering king as a show of triumph and superiority over the defeated king. In the same way, people from every nation and language, won out of Satan's one-world empire, will be at the throne of God, serving Him day and night forever in the New Jerusalem. Satan, the defeated king, will have lost this multitude of people out of the nations that he possessed. Jesus Christ will take them away captive. Jesus Christ is the conquering King and all those people will be His trophy of victory. When earthly kings took royal captives to make them slaves, it often was a sorrowful and demeaning experience. When God takes someone captive as a slave, however, it is all blessing. This multitude of people will continually have the best place in all the new creation forever. Being present at the throne of God and the Lamb will be the most awesome experience. People will not be able to get enough of it. Those captives who come out of the great tribulation will never have to leave the throne of God because it will be their place of privileged service, the reward for their faithfulness in washing their robes in the blood of the Lamb in the most troubled time of human history. God will spread His tabernacle over them. This is not a physical building. God and the Lamb are the temple and tabernacle in the New Jerusalem, Revelation 21:22. In the Old Testament period, nobody was allowed into the tabernacle and temple of God except the Levites of the tribe of Israel, Numbers 18:22–23. The presence of a gentile in the temple profaned the holy place of God, Ezekiel 44:6–10. But in the New Jerusalem, the servants of the tabernacle will not be an exclusive tribe or an exclusive race. The servants of the tabernacle will be people from all the nations. This will be an eternal testimony and reminder of the abundant love of God. This miracle of God will result in Him being eternally praised by angels and humans for the salvation He has graciously provided.

> And they cried out in a loud voice: "Salvation belongs to our God, who sits on the throne, and to the Lamb." All the angels were standing around the throne and around the elders and the four living creatures. They fell down on their faces before the throne and worshiped God, saying: "praise and glory and wisdom and thanks and honor and power and strength be to our God for ever and ever. Amen!"
>
> Revelation 7:10–12 (NASB)

In the New Jerusalem, there will be no physical building for a temple, and the radiant light of God will illuminate the whole city.

> And I saw no temple in it, for the Lord God, the Almighty, and the Lamb, are its temple. And the city has no need of the sun or of the moon to shine upon it, for the glory of God has illumined it, and its lamp is the Lamb.
>
> Revelation 21:22–23 (NASB)

Within the context of Revelation 21 and 22, "God" refers to the Father, and "Lamb" refers to Jesus Christ. God, the Father, and Jesus Christ, the Lamb, will eternally illuminate the New Jerusalem. This would appear to be saying that the radiant glory of the Father will be greater than that of the Lamb, who will be as a lamp. This could be interpreted that the kingdom of Jesus Christ has ended, and the new heaven and the new earth are the kingdom of the Father alone. That would contradict the many prophecies that the kingdom of Christ is eternal.

> I kept looking in the night visions, and behold, with the clouds of heaven One like a Son of Man was coming, and He came up to the Ancient of Days and was presented before Him. And to Him was given dominion, glory and a kingdom, that all the peoples, nations, and men of every language might serve Him. His dominion is an everlasting dominion which will not pass away; and His kingdom is one which will not be destroyed.
>
> Daniel 7:13–14 (NASB)

In the New Jerusalem, there is one throne, singular, and it is occupied by both God and the Lamb, from which the river of the water of life, the Holy Spirit, flows. In Revelation 11:15 the heavenly host sings, "The kingdom of this world has become the kingdom of our Lord, and of His Christ, and He will reign forever and ever." "He will reign" refers to both Father and Son because the Father and the Son are One. The kingdom and absolute dominion belong to the Father and His Christ. In human thinking, it would be right for Jesus to be the sole possessor of the kingdom because Jesus is the One who has done all the work. Jesus is the One who created all things and continually upholds all things by the Word of His power, Hebrews 1:2–3. Jesus is the One who emptied Himself of His deity and came into the world in the form of a man and suffered and died on a cross for the sins of the world, Philippians 2:5–8. It seems that the glory of the Lamb should illuminate the New Jerusalem and that God the Father should be the Lamp. That is the way fallen humans would handle the situation. But God's ways are not human ways and God's thoughts are not human thoughts, Isaiah 55:8–9. The selfish human perspective fails to grasp and totally overlooks the manifestation of the infinite and eternal divine love that exists between the Father, Son, and Holy Spirit. The Son performs all just as the Father has planned because of His unfathomable love for the Father. The Father loves the Son with an immeasurable love, giving Him a name above every name. At the very mention of His name every knee of all who are in heaven and on the earth and in the earth will bow, Philippians 2:10. The Father will cause every tongue to confess that Jesus Christ is Lord. Magnifying the glory and the name of Jesus Christ in this way is to the glory of God the Father. The Father is making all His enemies to be a footstool for the feet of Jesus Christ. The Father has given to the Son all authority over all the nations as His possession for His eternal kingdom. But in the New Jerusalem, Jesus Christ lovingly will give everything back to the Father so that the Father will be "all in all," which is the pinnacle of absolute dominion.

> Then comes the end, when He [Jesus] delivers up the kingdom to the God and Father, when He [the Father] has abolished all rule and all authority and power. For He [Jesus] must reign until He [the Father] has put all His enemies under His feet. The last enemy that will be abolished is death. For He [the Father] has put all things in subjection under His [Jesus] feet. But when He [the Father] says, "All things are put in subjection," it is evident that He [the Father] is excepted who put all things in subjection to Him [Jesus]. And when all things are subjected to Him [Jesus], then the Son Himself also will be subjected to the One who subjected all things to Him [Jesus], that God [the Father] may be all in all.
>
> 1 Corinthians 15:24–28 (NASB)

The words in square brackets are added for clarification of the pronouns. Ultimately God the Father will be the all in all. That means all dominion will belong to Him. God the Father will not be subjected to the Son, but the Son willfully subjects Himself to the Father, as He has always done. All these interchanges between the Father and the Son are expressions of eternal, infinite, divine love. While His Messiah reigns on the earth for one thousand years, the Father will remain seated in the third heaven.

During those thousand years, the Father will still be in the process of putting the enemies of Jesus Christ under His feet, bringing all things into subjection to Him and abolishing all other rule, authority, and power. The thousand-year messianic kingdom will begin with a sparse human population and everyone on the earth being a believer, but not all of them will be obedient.

> The Lord says to my Lord: "Sit at My right hand, until I make Thine enemies a footstool for Thy feet." The Lord will stretch forth Thy strong scepter from Zion, saying, "Rule in the midst of Thine enemies."
>
> Psalm 110:1–2 (NASB)

The earth will be quickly repopulated with peoples of all the nations through the thousand years. Many of those born during that time will reject the King, Jesus Christ, and will rebel against Him after Satan is released from the abyss. The final act of God the Father in bringing all into submission to Jesus Christ will be to rain fire from heaven to destroy these last enemies, Revelation 20:9.

In addition to all authority, the Father has given all judgment over to the Son. Jesus Christ will give a voice command and all who remain in the grave will come forth and be judged by Him.

> For not even the Father judges anyone, but He has given all judgment to the Son, in order that all may honor the Son, even as they honor the Father. He who does not honor the Son does not honor the Father who sent Him. Truly,

truly, I say to you, he who hears My word, and believes Him who sent Me, has eternal life, and does not come into judgment, but has passed out of death into life. Truly, truly, I say to you, an hour is coming and now is, when the dead shall hear the voice of the Son of God; and those who hear shall live. For just as the Father has life in Himself, even so He gave to the Son also to have life in Himself; and He gave Him authority to execute judgment, because He is the Son of Man. Do not marvel at this; for an hour is coming, in which all who are in the tombs shall hear His voice, and shall come forth; those who did the good deeds to a resurrection of life, those who committed the evil deeds to a resurrection of judgment. I can do nothing on My own initiative. As I hear, I judge; and My judgment is just, because I do not seek My own will, but the will of Him who sent Me.

John 5:22–30 (NASB)

Judgment by the Son will be in complete agreement with judgment by the Father. As the Father sentenced Satan and the fallen angels to the eternal lake of fire, so also Jesus Christ will sentence to the lake of fire all humans whose names have not been recorded in the Lamb's book of life from the foundation of the world.

And I saw a great white throne and Him who sat upon it, from whose presence earth and heaven fled away, and no place was found for them. And I saw the dead, the great and the small, standing before the throne, and books were opened; and another book was opened, which is the book of life; and the dead were judged from the things which were written in the books, according to their deeds. And the sea gave up the dead which were in it, and death and Hades gave up the dead which were in them; and they were judged, every one of them according to their deeds. And death and Hades were thrown into the lake of fire.

This is the second death, the lake of fire. And if anyone's name was not found written in the book of life, he was thrown into the lake of fire.

Revelation 20:11–15 (NASB)

After the great white throne judgment, all will finally be in total subjection to the Son. But all will not yet be completed.

Finally, Jesus Christ will then bring forth a new creation void of any corruption. The new creation will be started much the same way the first creation began. All the children of God will rejoice and have great celebration as they watch Jesus Christ put the new creation into place as the angelic host watched Him speak the original creation into existence, Job 38:4–7. The Father will join the Son on the new earth in the New Jerusalem and the Lamb will then yield to God so He will be "all in all," the final authority with absolute dominion over all creation forever and ever. Philippians 2:6 says that Jesus did not consider equality with God a thing to grasp. This mentality of Jesus Christ continues even into the eternal estate. The Son is equal to the Father, but out of love He is willing to yield to the Father. This act by Jesus Christ is the exact opposite of the actions of Lucifer that started the whole war for dominion. By this loving act of the Son toward the Father, the war for dominion will be over forever.

John writes in Revelation 21:23 that the New Jerusalem has no need for the sun or the moon to shine light upon it because God is its illumination and the Lamb is its lamp. This does not mean, however, that there won't be a sun and a moon in the new heavens. Isaiah says that there will be new moons and Sabbaths when there is the new heaven and the new earth.

"For just as the new heavens and the new earth which I make will endure before Me," declares the Lord, "So your offspring and your name will endure. And it shall be from new moon to new moon and from sabbath to sabbath, all mankind will come to bow down before Me," says the Lord.

Isaiah 66:22–23 (NASB)

In order for the moon to go through its phases, there must also be a sun along with the new earth. Also, God compares the permanency of the throne of David with the eternal nature of the sun and the moon.

> Once I have sworn by My holiness; I will not lie to David. His descendants shall endure forever, and his throne as the sun before Me. It shall be established forever like the moon, and the witness in the sky is faithful. [Selah]
>
> Psalm 89:35–37 (NASB)

The sun and the moon were in the original creation. They will be in the new creation as it is restored back to its original state. Therefore, when the Apostle John writes that there will be "no need" for the light of the sun and the moon to shine on the New Jerusalem, it does not say that they won't shine light on it. The light of God from the New Jerusalem will illuminate the area of the earth around the Holy Mountain. The rest of the earth will not be illuminated by the light of God and will have need for the sunlight.

> Then the moon will be abashed and the sun ashamed, for the Lord of hosts will reign on Mount Zion and in Jerusalem, and His glory will be before His elders.
>
> Isaiah 24:23 (NASB)

> And the light of the moon will be as the light of the sun, and the light of the sun will be seven times brighter, like the light of seven days, on the day the Lord binds up the fracture of His people and heals the bruise He has inflicted.
>
> Isaiah 30:26 (NASB)

> No longer will you have the sun for light by day, nor for
> brightness will the moon give you light; but you will have
> the Lord for an everlasting light, and your God for your
> glory. Your sun will set no more, neither will your moon
> wane; for you will have the Lord for an everlasting light,
> and the days of your mourning will be finished.
>
> Isaiah 60:19–20 (NASB)

These prophecies are not about the thousand-year kingdom
because the people in their flesh bodies on the earth would not
be able to approach Mt. Zion if the radiance of the glory of Jesus
Christ is seven times brighter than the sun. For the moon to be
abashed and the sun ashamed in the eternal estate, they have to
be in existence. When the new earth rotates so the sun shines on
the New Jerusalem, the light of God will be seven times more
radiant than the sun. When the new earth rotates so the New
Jerusalem is away from the sun then God the Father will dim
His radiant light that is brighter than the sun and the glory of
the Lamb will illuminate the New Jerusalem with a beautiful
radiant glow as a lamp that has the intensity of the sun. The light
of a lamp and the light of the moon are for light at night time,
Genesis 1:16. The glory of the Lamb shining out of the New
Jerusalem at night will be an eternal reminder that He came as
the Light shining into darkness.

> In Him was life, and the life was the light of men. And
> the light shines in the darkness, and the darkness did not
> comprehend it.
>
> John 1:4–5 (NASB)

The light of the Lamb being the lamp does not mean that God's
radiance will outshine that of the Lamb. In an awesome and
beautiful display, both God and the Lamb will each have their
time of the day to show forth their eternal and glorious light out

through the eternal city and into the world. Truly Israel's sun will never set, and their moon will never wane as the everlasting light of the Lord and glory of God will eternally illuminate all Israel on the new earth. The New Jerusalem will be surrounded by a wall seventy-two yards high made of jasper. The city is made of pure gold, transparent like glass, with a foundation stone adorned with precious jewels, Revelation 21:17–20. The radiant light of God and the Lamb shining forth from the New Jerusalem will make it brilliant like a very costly stone, Revelation 21:11. Day and night, for all eternity, the New Jerusalem is going to be an amazingly beautiful place to behold. The city will be fifteen hundred miles in height, width, and length, Revelation 21:16. If the throne of God and the Lamb is at the center of the city that means their radiant light has to emanate seven hundred and fifty miles in every direction to shine out through the transparent gold walls with intensity greater than the light of the sun. Human eyes in their current state are not able to look upon such radiant light, as Paul experienced, Acts 9:3–8. In our resurrection bodies, we will be able to look upon the radiant manifestation of the glory of God and the Lamb.

Right now the church resides in the kingdom of darkness. The earth is occupied by people who love the darkness and hate the light, John 3:19–20. But God is going to remove the darkness and replace it with the kingdom of light.

> Arise, shine; for your light has come, and the glory of the Lord has risen upon you. For behold, darkness will cover the earth, and deep darkness the peoples; but the Lord will rise upon you, and His glory will appear upon you. And nations will come to your light, and kings to the brightness of your rising.
>
> Isaiah 60:1–3 (NASB)

Fulfillment of this prophecy begins in the thousand-year kingdom of Jesus Christ and then continues on the new earth with an intensity of light beyond our comprehension. The kings and the nations on the new earth will bring the glory of the nations into the New Jerusalem. Though we temporarily reside in the kingdom of darkness, our home is in the kingdom of the light of Jesus Christ.

> For He delivered us from the domain of darkness, and transferred us to the kingdom of His beloved Son, in whom we have redemption, the forgiveness of sins.
>
> Colossians 1:13–14 (NASB)

We have suffering, trials, tribulations, and death in the kingdom of darkness, but we have the promise of great eternal blessings to come.

> Therefore we do not lose heart, but though our outer man is decaying, yet our inner man is being renewed day by day. For momentary, light affliction is producing for us an eternal weight of glory far beyond all comparison, while we look not at the things which are seen, but at the things which are not seen; for the things which are seen are temporal, but the things which are not seen are eternal.
>
> 2 Corinthians 4:16–18 (NASB)

All these things will be fully realized when God has taken total dominion over all creation and reigns eternally from the New Jerusalem. All will be in total subjection to Him, and there will be no end of His dominion. It will be an existence beyond anything we are able to comprehend at the present time. Thanks be to the Father, the Lamb, and the Holy Spirit for their unfathomable love, mercy, and grace given to us.

In the original creation, Jesus Christ created the Holy Mountain on the earth as the abode of the Father. From there the Father reigned over all that was created by Jesus Christ. When the Father takes the throne in the New Jerusalem, it will be for the first time since the fall of Lucifer that He has reigned over the creation from the earth.

> And I heard a loud voice from the throne, saying, "Behold, the tabernacle of God is among men, and He shall dwell among them, and they shall be His people, and God Himself shall be among them."
>
> Revelation 21:3 (NASB)

The loud voice from the throne is the voice of the Father expressing His great pleasure. God has an overwhelming zeal and love for His Holy Mountain, desiring to return there.

> Thus says the Lord of hosts, "I am exceedingly jealous for Zion, yes, with great wrath I am jealous for her." Thus says the Lord, "I will return to Zion and will dwell in the midst of Jerusalem. Then Jerusalem will be called the City of Truth, and the mountain of the Lord of hosts will be called the Holy Mountain."
>
> Zechariah 8:2–3 (NASB)

The Father's renewed reign from the Holy Mountain will be a reign of eternal divine love.

> And He shall wipe away every tear from their eyes; and there shall no longer be any death; there shall no longer be any mourning, or crying, or pain; the first things have passed away. And He who sits on the throne said, "Behold, I am making all things new." And He said, "Write, for these words are faithful and true." And He said to me, "It

is done. I am the Alpha and the Omega, the beginning and the end. I will give to the one who thirsts from the spring of the water of life without cost."

Revelation 21:4–6 (NASB)

The Father will give freely to His eternal children the water of life, the Holy Spirit. According to the prophecy in Ezekiel 47, in the thousand-year kingdom of Christ, two rivers will flow from the temple on Mt. Zion. One will flow toward the east and one toward the west. Scripture does not say for certain, but the River of Life could possibly flow from the New Jerusalem, down the Holy Mountain, and throughout the new earth as springs of living water. God, the all in all, is the loving Father who will wipe away every tear and will take away the curse of physical death so that all mourning, pain, and crying are passed away forever. When God finally reestablishes His Holy Mountain on the new earth, His creation will never again become corrupted by sin of the created beings. Sin is the cause of death, tears, mourning, crying, and pain. Because these will never exist again, there can never again be sin and rebellion against the Creator. The Father makes all things new through Jesus Christ, as He made the first creation through Jesus Christ, Hebrews 1:2. God the Father is the Alpha and the Omega speaking in Revelation 21:6, and Jesus Christ is the Alpha and the Omega speaking in Revelation 22:13 and 16. Both the Father and the Son rightfully carry this title.

> Thus saith the LORD the King of Israel, and his redeemer the LORD of hosts; I am the first, and I am the last; and beside me there is no God.

Isaiah 44:6 (NASB)

As God will be most pleased when the New Jerusalem is established on the new Holy Mountain on the earth, so also the Lamb will be most pleased.

> And I saw the holy city, new Jerusalem, coming down out of heaven from God, made ready as a bride adorned for her husband.
>
> Revelation 21:2 (NASB)

Jesus Christ has been constructing the New Jerusalem as the eternal abode for His bride since He ascended to heaven forty days after His resurrection. When it is completed Jesus Christ will return to take His bride off the earth.

> In My Father's house are many dwelling places; if it were not so, I would have told you; for I go to prepare a place for you. And if I go and prepare a place for you, I will come again, and receive you to Myself; that where I am, there you may be also. And you know the way where I am going.
>
> John 14:2–4 (NASB)

The house of the Father and the place Jesus prepares for His bride and the New Jerusalem are all the same place. When Jesus comes and receives His bride to Himself, the bride will be with Him forever, 1 Thessalonians 4:17. The Lamb and His bride will not immediately occupy the place Jesus has prepared. The bride will first reign with Christ on the earth for one thousand years, which is covered in more depth in the chapter "Dominion of the Faithful." After the thousand years and the creation of the new heaven and the new earth, the Father will move the New Jerusalem from the third heaven to the new earth.

> And one of the seven angels who had the seven bowls full of the seven last plagues, came and spoke with me,

saying, "Come here, I shall show you the bride, the wife of the Lamb." And he carried me away in the Spirit to a great and high mountain, and showed me the holy city, Jerusalem, coming down out of heaven from God.

Revelation 21:9–10 (NASB)

And I saw the holy city, new Jerusalem, coming down out of heaven from God, made ready as a bride adorned for her husband.

Revelation 21:2 (NASB)

Note the difference: Revelation 21:2 says the New Jerusalem appears "as a bride adorned for her husband," and Revelation 21:9 calls the New Jerusalem "the bride, the wife of the Lamb." The marriage between the Lamb and His bride will be consummated in the New Jerusalem, so she will go from being His bride to being the Lamb's wife. When Jesus Christ sees the New Jerusalem occupied by His bride coming to the new earth, it will be to Him like a groom seeing his bride coming down the aisle. When a man builds a home for his bride, the home is not complete until she takes up residence in the home as his wife. The New Jerusalem will finally be complete. The physical structure of the New Jerusalem is not the bride. What makes the New Jerusalem to be the bride of the Lamb is the residing presence of His beloved bride. The procession of the New Jerusalem from heaven to the new earth will no doubt be accompanied by a great celebration. God will finally achieve His purpose in the new creation, fulfilling the desire He has had since the original creation. God says, "I will rejoice."

For behold, I create new heavens and a new earth; and the former things shall not be remembered or come to mind. But be glad and rejoice forever in what I create; for behold, I create Jerusalem for rejoicing, and her people for gladness. I will also rejoice in Jerusalem, and be glad in My people; And there will no longer be heard in her the voice of weeping and the sound of crying.

Isaiah 65:17–19 (NASB)

ETERNAL REWARDS

The intention of the previous chapters of this book has been to show the past, present, and future of God's plan to be the sole possessor of all rule, authority and dominion in His creation. The remaining chapters will reveal how Christians can share that dominion with Christ in His coming eternal and glorious kingdom and why God wants to give us this blessing.

God's purpose for His creation is the existence of created beings He can love and who will choose to love Him in return. This purpose necessitated that God create beings with free-choice ability, which resulted in an undesirable and unwanted challenge to God's rule, authority, and dominion. If God had not created beings possessing free will, there would never have been a need for God to assert His absolute rule and authority over His creation. But without the love of free-will beings, God's purpose for the creation would not be achieved. God wants both the dominion and the love. God is willing to make every sacrifice necessary to achieve His desire, including the love sacrifice made by God the Son on the cross to pay the entire penalty for every human misuse and abuse of the gift of free-choice ability graciously given to them as a blessing. God has made the weak and frail human race to fulfill a very important role in His plan to possess absolute dominion in His creation purposed to be a place for eternal love relationships. After one-third of the angels chose to rebel, God created the human male and female in His own image and then created the animals as a living illustration of love, free-choice ability, and dominion. When the man and the woman chose to rebel, they lost the dominion that God had entrusted to them, and they lost the ability of pure and undefiled love, which God defines as self-sacrifice. Humans became self-serving lovers of self in their fallen nature.

> The heart is more deceitful than all else and is desperately sick; Who can understand it?
>
> Jeremiah 17:9 (NASB)

As Christians we have the opportunity, after salvation, to be transformed back to possessing the character of God as creatures full of love in our inner beings and having a place of high authority in Jesus Christ while still in this temporal life. But for this to happen, our old-flesh natures have to be sacrificed. We are again faced with a choice between clinging to our old fallen natures or letting God put our old fallen natures to death so the the new creation that He birthed in each of us at salvation can mature to become the dominant character.

> Jesus answered and said to him, "Truly, truly, I say to you, unless one is born again, he cannot see the kingdom of God."
>
> John 3:3 (NASB)

> Jesus answered, "Truly, truly, I say to you, unless one is born of water and the Spirit, he cannot enter into the kingdom of God. That which is born of the flesh is flesh, and that which is born of the Spirit is spirit."
>
> John 3:5–6 (NASB)

The birth that is of the flesh is our physical birth, and the birth of the Spirit is the birth of the new creation. At spiritual birth we are suddenly changed inside from possessing one nature to possessing two natures, the old-flesh nature and the new spiritual being. Like an infant, the new spiritual creation has to be fed to mature and grow.

> That you put off, concerning your former conduct, the old man which grows corrupt according to the deceitful lusts, and be renewed in the spirit of your mind, and that you put on the new man which was created according to God, in true righteousness and holiness.
>
> Ephesians 4:22–24 (NKJV)

The old-flesh self is not and cannot be made to be true, righteous, and holy. When we consistently feed our new selves on the Word of God, the new man becomes the dominant character in us. The outside change will come later at the resurrection. But right now the new self can become stronger and more alive every day.

> Therefore we do not lose heart, but though our outer man is decaying, yet our inner man is being renewed day by day.
>
> 2 Corinthians 4:16 (NASB)

Christians who choose to be matured as new spiritual beings will be given eternal rewards of sharing in the eternal kingdom of Jesus Christ. The dominion that Satan has sought to obtain by rebellion and force, Christians can obtain by love for God through obedience. It glorifies God to be able to give rewards to Christians. God will be successful in achieving His goal of love and dominion, and Christians have the opportunity to share in His victory. The coming dominion of Christ on this earth is a glorious period in the plan of God. Even more glorious will be the coming glory of the new heaven, the new earth, and the

New Jerusalem, which are eternal, without end. Each member of the body of Christ has the opportunity in this temporal life to gain the reward of sharing in the glorious dominion of the coming kingdom age of Jesus Christ and the eternal estate. The opportunity to gain eternal rewards will never come again for all eternity. The rewards are eternal, but the only opportunity to acquire them is now in this temporal life. The way that we live our temporal lives on this earth after salvation is God's basis for giving and withholding eternal rewards.

The pursuit of eternal rewards is not the same as the fleshly ambition driving the pursuit of worldly possessions and power.

> But godliness actually is a means of great gain, when accompanied by contentment. For we have brought nothing into the world, so we cannot take anything out of it either. And if we have food and covering, with these we shall be content. But those who want to get rich fall into temptation and a snare and many foolish and harmful desires which plunge men into ruin and destruction. For the love of money is a root of all sorts of evil, and some by longing for it have wandered away from the faith, and pierced themselves with many a pang.
>
> 1 Timothy 6:6-10 (NASB)

The "great gain" from godliness far exceeds any worldly gains that can be acquired through the works of the flesh. God will give no eternal rewards for the fleshly works that involve the selfish pursuit of temporal worldly wealth and power. Eternal rewards can be obtained only through self-sacrifice, which is the exact opposite of selfish ambition. Jesus Christ was motivated by the promise of reward.

> Fixing our eyes on Jesus, the author and perfecter of faith, who for the joy set before Him endured the cross,

despising the shame, and has sat down at the right hand of the throne of God.

Hebrews 12:2 (NASB)

So also God has set a joy and promise of reward before Christians.

But just as it is written, "THINGS WHICH EYE HAS NOT SEEN AND EAR HAS NOT HEARD, AND WHICH HAVE NOT ENTERED THE HEART OF MAN, ALL THAT GOD HAS PREPARED FOR THOSE WHO LOVE HIM."

1 Corinthians 2:9 (NASB)

God put a qualifier on this promise, "for those who love Him." The believer's pursuit to draw closer into a personal love relationship with Jesus Christ and the pursuit of eternal rewards are one and the same. Because this pursuit involves becoming a bond slave empowered by the Holy Spirit, the motivation is the exact opposite of the self-promoting works of the flesh nature that feed delusions of grandeur. The concept of rewards can be confusing because it conveys the idea that we can earn or deserve something from God. This seems to conflict with the concept of God's grace and mercy, where grace is the bestowing of blessings we do not deserve and mercy is withholding of punishment we do deserve. But God's loving character of forgiveness and abounding grace is not nullified by His giving of rewards and commendations. Give thanks to God that He is patient and merciful beyond anything we can comprehend.

Bless the Lord, O my soul; And all that is within me, bless His holy name. Bless the Lord, O my soul, And forget none of His benefits; Who pardons all your iniquities; Who heals all your diseases; Who redeems your life from the pit; Who crowns you with lovingkindness and compassion.

Psalm 103:1–4 (NASB)

Let the wicked forsake his way, and the unrighteous man his thoughts; And let him return to the Lord, and He will have compassion on him; and to our God, for He will abundantly pardon.

Isaiah 55:7 (NASB)

Truly our God is ready to forgive and restore anyone who comes to Him making confession of their sin with repentant hearts. Every child of God has need for His compassion even after salvation because no child of God walks in sinless perfection in this life.

If we say that we have no sin, we are deceiving ourselves, and the truth is not in us.

1 John 1:8 (NASB)

God called King David a man after His own heart, and he was the righteous standard by which the other kings of Judah and Israel were measured, 1 Kings 9:4–5 and 2 Kings 18:3. Yet even David knew that he was just like all the rest of the human race, desperately needing God to deal with him in mercy and grace.

And do not enter into judgment with Thy servant, for in Thy sight no man living is righteous.

Psalm 143:2 (NASB)

Sin continues to be a reality in every believer's temporal life after salvation. Truly the death of Jesus Christ removed the consequences of our sins with regard to our eternal destinies. Every day in our temporal lives, however, we must still deal with the consequences of the suffering, pain, and hurt caused by our sins. The death of Jesus Christ did not remove the consequences of our sins in this temporal life. But Jesus Christ did not leave us as orphans, abandoned to continually wallow in the misery of sin.

> If you love Me, you will keep My commandments. And I will ask the Father, and He will give you another Helper, that He may be with you forever; that is the Spirit of truth, whom the world cannot receive, because it does not behold Him or know Him, but you know Him because He abides with you, and will be in you. I will not leave you as orphans; I will come to you.
>
> John 14:15–18 (NASB)

Jesus prayed to the Father that He would send the Holy Spirit to those men and ultimately to all the church. The Holy Spirit is the One who enables us to keep His commandments, while the flesh nature inside of us wants to do everything but keep God's commandments.

> But I say, walk by the Spirit, and you will not carry out the desire of the flesh. For the flesh sets its desire against the Spirit, and the Spirit against the flesh; for these are in opposition to one another, so that you may not do the things that you please.
>
> Galatians 5:16–17 (NASB)

God has given us His Holy Spirit to battle our flesh natures with the goal that we avoid sin and are able to more consistently abide in the light with Him. The focus of every child of God needs to be a vigilance to walk in the light as He is in the light so as to have fellowship with Him.

> And this is the message we have heard from Him and announce to you, that God is light, and in Him there is no darkness at all. If we say that we have fellowship with Him and yet walk in the darkness, we lie and do not practice the truth.
>
> 1 John 1:5–6 (NASB)

Amazingly, even with the Holy Spirit residing in us, we still fail in sin. But we have not been left helpless in our sins in this life. God has made a provision that enables us to keep returning to the light after we have wandered astray into the darkness by sin. In addition to making the sacrifice of Jesus Christ our way to eternal life, God has also graciously made Jesus' sacrifice the means whereby we can deal with our sins on a moment by moment basis, thus enabling our quick return to having fellowship in His light.

> But if we walk in the light as He Himself is in the light, we have fellowship with one another, and the blood of Jesus His Son cleanses us from all sin.
>
> If we confess our sins, He is faithful and righteous to forgive us our sins and to cleanse us from all unrighteousness.
>
> 1 John 1:7 and 9 (NASB)

> My little children, I am writing these things to you that you may not sin. And if anyone sins, we have an Advocate with the Father, Jesus Christ the righteous;
>
> 1 John 2:1 (NASB)

The goal is that we not sin. But when believers do sin, it is by the most precious blood of our Advocate that we are continually cleansed of the filth of our sins in this temporal life so we can return to walking in the light. But to receive this mercy we must go to Him in confession and repentance.

Not only is Jesus Christ our Advocate, but He is also our High Priest ready to help us in any temptation we face.

> For we do not have a high priest who is unable to sympathize with our weaknesses, but we have one who has been tempted in every way, just as we are—yet was without sin. Let us therefore draw near with confidence to the throne of grace, that we may receive mercy and may find grace to help in time of need.
>
> Hebrews 4:15–16 (NASB)

> For since He Himself was tempted in that which He has suffered, He is able to come to the aid of those who are tempted.
>
> Hebrews 2:18 (NASB)

> No temptation has overtaken you but such as is common to man; and God is faithful, who will not allow you to be tempted beyond what you are able, but with the temptation will provide the way of escape also, that you may be able to endure it.
>
> 1 Corinthians 10:13 (NASB)

The "throne of grace" is not the place believers go to ask for material blessings of this life. The grace we need is sympathy and help for our weaknesses in times of temptation, which is much more valuable than any worldly possession. If we let the High Priest strengthen us so that we can prevail over temptations, it will result in eternal rewards and blessings of eternal possessions. Believers who go to the throne of grace asking for temporal possessions are very shortsighted. Jesus Christ is our High Priest waiting to strengthen us and to enable us to be obedient to the Father. If we are quick to go to Jesus as our High Priest, we will be more likely to avoid having to go to Him as our Advocate.

Jesus faced every temptation that we can encounter, and He did it without sinning. Therefore, He knows the way for us to escape the temptation to sin. As our High Priest, Jesus is always ready and waiting to help us in our time of need because He does not want us to sin. The High Priest wants us to come to Him with "confidence" that He will provide the "way of escape" just as He has promised. Most often the way of escape that Jesus provides is the Holy Spirit that God has given to live inside each believer. It is crucial that we continually go to the throne of grace seeking the help and power of our High Priest when we are tempted. But it is also vital that believers go to the Advocate in confession and repentance when having failed in sin.

> But if we judged ourselves rightly, we should not be judged. But when we are judged, we are disciplined by the Lord in order that we may not be condemned along with the world.
>
> 1 Corinthians 11:31–32 (NASB)

In the context of this verse, Paul is addressing believers who were taking the Lord's Supper in an unworthy manner, which means taking communion while living in the flesh and walking in darkness. But the principle of rightly judging ourselves is applicable to every aspect of our lives. Rightly judging ourselves is an inherent part of going to the Advocate in confession and repentance in order to be restored to walking in the light. Those who fail to continually seek this grace of God now are storing up judgment for themselves later at the judgment seat of Jesus Christ.

> For we must all appear before the judgment seat of Christ, that each one may be recompensed for his deeds in the body, according to what he has done, whether good or bad.
>
> 2 Corinthians 5:10 (NASB)

This is written to believers, not unbelievers. Believers' works are judged to determine their recompense of eternal rewards, or lack thereof. Unbelievers' works are judged to determine if they are good enough to escape the lake of fire, which no unbeliever will escape, Revelation 20:11-5. In 1 Corinthians the Apostle Paul gives more information about the judgment of believers, those having the foundation of Jesus Christ.

> For no man can lay a foundation other than the one which is laid, which is Jesus Christ. Now if any man builds upon the foundation with gold, silver, precious stones, wood, hay, straw, each man's work will become evident; for the day will show it, because it is to be revealed with fire; and the fire itself will test the quality of each man's work. If any man's work which he has built upon it remains, he shall receive a reward. If any man's work is burned up, he shall suffer loss; but he himself shall be saved, yet so as through fire.
>
> 1 Corinthians 3:11–15 (NASB)

The believer's foundation of Jesus Christ is not burned up by the testing fire, but only the works built on the foundation. This judgment is not an evaluation of our works before salvation, but our works as Christians after salvation.

> For by grace you have been saved through faith; and that not of yourselves, it is the gift of God; not as a result of works, that no one should boast. For we are His workmanship, created in Christ Jesus for good works, which God prepared beforehand, that we should walk in them.
>
> Ephesians 2:8–10 (NASB)

All human works done prior to receiving the gift of salvation are worthless and discarded. It is only by the grace of God that anyone can be saved. It has to be given as a gift, which can be received only by faith. But God has prepared good works for us to do after salvation. "We should walk in them," but not every believer does. Those are the works of believers that Jesus Christ will judge, whether good or bad, and they are the basis on which the Lord gives us eternal rewards. The works of the faithful believer will be so valuable to our Lord that He calls them gold, silver, and precious stones. These works will be greatly rewarded. Our bad works are totally of no value to our Lord like wood, hay, and straw. They will be incinerated by the Lord at His judgment seat. If our works after salvation endure the Lord's testing fire, then we will receive rewards. We will all have some wood, hay, and straw that will be destroyed. The more bad works that a believer has, the bigger the fire and the more eternal rewards that believer will lose. Believers who have spent their temporal lives after salvation continually living in the flesh will have all their works burned up. Those unfaithful believers will "suffer loss" of rewards, though they themselves are saved to eternal life. Paul uses the word *suffer*, meaning the experience of "loss" will be unpleasant. The loss is eternal. The Lord will not give anyone a chance to redo it. To be "saved yet so as through fire" is not going to be a joyful experience. However, at the very least, the unfaithful believers have the foundation of Jesus Christ. Everyone who receives by faith the gift of being saved by grace is immediately established on the foundation of Jesus Christ. The solid foundation of Jesus Christ is not burned and destroyed out from under them by the testing fire. Only the fleshly works built upon the foundation are destroyed. Bad works after salvation do not result in any believer being cast into the lake of fire, "but he himself shall be saved."

We each have the opportunity now in this temporal life to go to God the Father with Jesus Christ as our Advocate to deal with our sins as His children. Or, we can let our sins pile up and have Jesus Christ deal with them all at once at His judgment seat where He will test the works of each believer with fire. The judgment seat will not be the time to start seeking His grace and mercy. Jesus Christ presides at both the throne of grace now and the judgment seat later, but His purpose and function are not the same. His position on the throne of grace is temporal while believers are living on the earth dealing with temptation that comes from the world, the devil, and their own flesh natures. His purpose and function is to help us deal with these enemies. When our time of living in these temporal bodies plagued with the flesh nature is over, there will be no more need for the throne of grace for us. Our time of trial and temptation will be over forever. The next step is the judgment seat where Jesus Christ will give out rewards and rebukes. Christians who have spent their lives boldly running to the throne of grace for help conquering sin will receive rewards when they stand at the judgment seat. Christians who have not been in attendance at the throne of grace will be plagued with sinful lives, and they will receive rebuke from Jesus Christ, and not rewards, when they stand at the judgment seat. It is essential that believers not confuse the purpose of the High Priest at the throne of grace with the purpose of Jesus Christ at the judgment seat. The time to seek the abundant mercy and grace of God is now. Those who have continually sought the aid of the High Priest and Advocate will have many deeds of walking in the light by the power of the Holy Spirit. These deeds will be rewarded. Those who disregard the High Priest and Advocate will have deeds of walking in the darkness by the energy of the flesh. These deeds will result in the loss of rewards. These things are most serious because a believer's life of disobedience now will have eternal ramifications; not loss of eternal life, but loss of marvelous and wonderful eternal rewards. The death of Jesus Christ on the cross procured our deliverance out of the lake of fire, but it did not procure for us our rewards and our status in the kingdom age and the eternal estate. The judgment seat will be a sorrowful place for members of the body of Christ who fail to use the gracious provisions of the Holy Spirit, the throne of grace of our High Priest, the local church, and the Holy Scriptures that God has given to us for this temporal life. Not only does our Advocate desire to intercede for us, but the Holy Spirit also desires to help us in our weaknesses.

> And in the same way the Spirit also helps our weakness; for we do not know how to pray as we should, but the Spirit Himself intercedes for us with groanings too deep for words; and He who searches the hearts knows what the mind of the Spirit is, because He intercedes for the saints according to the will of God.
>
> Romans 8:26–27 (NASB)

The context of Romans 8 is the inner struggle between the flesh nature and the Holy Spirit that we all experience. The Spirit intercedes for us with groaning regarding the weaknesses of our flesh nature. The Holy Spirit and the High Priest both want us to have the victory. With all the divine assets given to us, no child of God should be continually walking in darkness. Walking in the darkness of the flesh and the world is misery. Believers who have experienced the joy of living in God's light are diligent to stay there. Some believers are babes in Christ while others have had decades of experience as believers. The Lord is full of patience and compassion wanting to relate to each believer according to their own level of maturity. It is a miracle that we are able to have a personal relationship with our Lord now while we live in bodies infested with flesh natures and in a dark world ruled by Satan. God's highest purpose for all His gracious provisions to the church is that each believer achieves a personal relationship with Him while in this temporal life. Those who truly want to know their Creator and Savior will make full use of these provisions. Our deeds after salvation are very revealing of the heart we each have for our Savior. Our Lord is able to look into the depths of our hearts to know the motivation for our deeds. Jesus Christ is able to discern those who truly desire to know Him. That will be the bottom line at His judgment seat for believers.

Our Lord is full of loving-kindness, but as His chosen people Israel have learned, He deals severely with those who deny Him the personal and intimate relationship of obedience He desires from us. In writing about the disobedience of Israel, Paul warns,

> Behold then the kindness and severity of God; to those who fell, severity, but to you, God's kindness, if you continue in His kindness; otherwise you also will be cut off.
>
> Romans 11:22 (NASB)

Being "cut off" does not mean loss of eternal life, but being deprived of God's blessings now and being denied the eternal blessings of rewards. The way that we walk in this temporal life establishes our eternal status in the kingdom of Jesus Christ and also in the new heaven and the new earth. We must all join with Paul in running the race and buffeting our bodies so that we won't be disqualified from receiving the rewards, which Paul refers to as an imperishable wreath.

> Therefore I run in such a way, as not without aim; I box in such a way, as not beating the air; but I buffet my body and make it my slave, lest possibly, after I have preached to others, I myself should be disqualified.
>
> 1 Corinthians 9:26–27 (NASB)

Paul is not talking about actual physical discipline of his physical body. He makes that clear in his letter to Timothy.

> On the other hand, discipline yourself for the purpose of godliness; for bodily discipline is only of little profit, but godliness is profitable for all things, since it holds promise for the present life and also for the life to come.
>
> 1 Timothy 4:7–8 (NASB)

When Paul writes about buffeting his body, he is actually referring to spiritual discipline which will result in the inheritance of eternal rewards "for the life to come." Buffeting the body is the battle that rages in our members. Paul clarifies this in his letter to the believers in Rome.

> For I joyfully concur with the law of God in the inner man, but I see a different law in the members of my body, waging war against the law of my mind, and making me a prisoner of the law of sin which is in my members.
>
> Romans 7:22–23 (NASB)

The church epistles clearly teach us that we have a battle to fight after salvation. The biggest part of that battle is inside our own selves. Believers must daily examine themselves to determine if they are relying on the grace of Jesus Christ and the power of the Holy Spirit. After salvation each believer is faced with the need to plan for the eternal future. The decisions we make about how to live our temporal lives after salvation will determine our eternal status in the new creation, and we will each live with those ramifications forever. Eternity is a long time. Jesus Christ paid a very high price for our salvation and He wants to be able to give each of us nothing but the best, which will be to His eternal glory. God does not want to have to punish us. The Lord would much rather bless now and reward us for all eternity.

> "But if the wicked man turns from all his sins which he has committed and observes all My statutes and practices justice and righteousness, he shall surely live; he shall not die. All his transgressions which he has committed will not be remembered against him; because of his righteousness which he has practiced, he will live. Do I have any pleasure in the death of the wicked," declares the Lord God, "rather than that he should turn from his ways and live?"
>
> Ezekiel 18:21–23 (NASB)

When Israel sinned, God punished many of them with physical death. God much more preferred that they would have repented so He could have blessed them, Luke 13:34. So also God takes no pleasure in having to punish us. Certainly Jesus Christ will take no pleasure in having to deny us eternal rewards at His judgment seat. But only believers who spend their temporal lives after salvation continually running to the "throne of grace" will receive the help and strength they need to walk in obedience to God. The power of God is graciously imparted to each believer as needed. The success of believers is not by their own strength. All the glory and the credit belong to Jesus Christ. He is our victory. When Jesus Christ is able give rewards at the judgment seat for believers, He will be piling grace upon the grace that He already gave to them when they came to His throne of grace in the temporal life. We will receive rewards for having received His grace. It glorifies the Lord to be able to give us the rewards. God's giving of rewards does correlate with God's mercy and grace which cannot be earned or deserved.

Many believers may think that losing eternal rewards is no big deal. They figure the loss is worth being able to satisfy their fleshly desires now, since they will still escape the eternal lake of fire. The Apostle John had a unique perspective of what the judgment seat of Christ will be like for the faithful versus the unfaithful.

> And as for you, the anointing which you received from Him abides in you, and you have no need for anyone to teach you; but as His anointing teaches you about all things, and is true and is not a lie, and just as it has taught you, you abide in Him. And now, little children, abide in Him, so that when He appears, we may have confidence and not shrink away from Him in shame at His coming.
>
> 1 John 2:27–28 (NASB)

The "anointing" is God the Holy Spirit given to live inside every believer. Those who live by the anointing will "have confidence" when Jesus Christ appears. Believers who do not live by the anointing will "shrink away from Him in shame" when Jesus Christ appears. Unfaithful believers will be looking for a place to hide, but there will be no place to run and no place to hide from Jesus Christ, and His judgment of every believer's works after salvation. In this passage, John reveals that believers who want to be confident at the appearance of Jesus Christ must be consistently receiving the teaching of the Holy Spirit, "His anointing teaches you about all things, and is true and is not a lie, and just as it has taught you, you abide in Him." The more the Holy Spirit teaches us, the more we are able to abide in Him, Jesus Christ. When He appears, we will be meeting someone we already know personally through the personal fellowship we have had with Him, which will give us confidence. Believers who fail to abide in Christ through the teaching of the Holy Spirit will meet a stranger when Christ appears. His holiness will suddenly become very real to them, and they will be convicted so they will want to shrink away. The Greek word translated *shrink away* means "shame, disgrace, cause of shame, dishonorable conduct."

God gives a real life account in His Word about someone who lost his inheritance and greatly regretted it afterward. Esau and Jacob were twins born to Isaac and Rebekah. Esau was born first so the family birthright of inheritance belonged to him. This inheritance included the promise God had made to Abraham and Isaac that God would bless them and make them a great nation and give their descendents the promised land. These things of God meant nothing to Esau because he easily traded them to Jacob for a bowl of stew to satisfy his temporal desire.

> And when Jacob had cooked stew, Esau came in from
> the field and he was famished; and Esau said to Jacob,

"Please let me have a swallow of that red stuff there, for I am famished." Therefore his name was called Edom. But Jacob said, "First sell me your birthright." And Esau said, "Behold, I am about to die; so of what use then is the birthright to me?" And Jacob said, "First swear to me"; so he swore to him, and sold his birthright to Jacob. Then Jacob gave Esau bread and lentil stew; and he ate and drank, and rose and went on his way. Thus Esau despised his birthright.

Genesis 25:29–34 (NASB)

As Esau craved the stew to fulfill his immediate hunger, so also many believers crave worldly things to immediately satisfy their fleshly desires, giving no regard to what eternal blessing of inheritance they might be giving up as a result. Jesus issues a warning to the Philadelphia church about this very thing.

I am coming quickly; hold fast what you have, in order that no one take your crown.

Revelation 3:11 (NASB)

This has the concept of someone distracting or deterring believers from their endeavor to obtain the crown. Within the context of this verse the ones deterring are those of the "synagogue of Satan," or the satanic force on earth. The spiritual powers of darkness want to distract us from our destiny. To receive the crowns and rewards as an eternal inheritance, we must "hold fast." We have to be diligent in our pursuit. Esau was not holding fast to the birthright, and he was not vigilant or concerned about losing it. The blessing of the firstborn rightfully belonged to Jacob after Esau willingly traded it for food. Jacob later ended up taking the birthright through deception because Esau was obviously going to renege on the deal when Isaac informed Esau he wanted to give him the blessing, Genesis 27:1–5. The birthright and the promises of God meant everything to Jacob to the extent that he was willing to do whatever was necessary, and he was diligent to seize any opportunity to acquire the blessing. That is the way we all need to be about gaining the inheritance of rewards that the Lord desires to give us at His judgment seat. When Esau found out that he had lost the inheritance, it suddenly became important to him. But it was too late, just as it will be too late for rebellious believers when they are told they have no inheritance at the judgment seat of Christ. Many of them will have the same sorrowful response.

> When Esau heard the words of his father, he cried out with an exceedingly great and bitter cry, and said to his father, "Bless me, even me also, O my father!"
> And Esau said to his father, "Do you have only one blessing, my father? Bless me, even me also, O my father." So Esau lifted his voice and wept.
>
> Genesis 27:34 and 38 (NASB)

> For you know that even afterwards, when he desired to inherit the blessing, he was rejected, for he found no place for repentance, though he sought for it with tears.
>
> Hebrews 12:17 (NASB)

It is very presumptuous for a believer to assume that it will be no big deal when they stand before the judgment seat of Christ and are denied eternal rewards. There will be repentance with tears, but their repentance will be too late to gain the inheritance. The rewards at the judgment seat of Jesus Christ are not going to be just tokens of appreciation like a twenty-year service pin from an employer. These are rewards from the sovereign One who possesses the whole universe. Paul tries to give us a concept of what the rewards will be like.

> For momentary, light affliction is producing for us an eternal weight of glory far beyond all comparison, while we look not at the things which are seen, but at the things which are not seen; for the things which are seen are temporal, but the things which are not seen are eternal.
>
> 2 Corinthians 4:17–18 (NASB)

Paul assures us that any sacrifice we could make is well worth the rewards. Certainly when the unfaithful believers see the unimaginable rewards that the faithful believers are given, the unfaithful will suddenly realize what they have missed, just as Esau suddenly realized what he had forfeited after it was gone.

Truly, there will be none who are on the new earth who will be disappointed to be there, but we must not let this be a rationale that causes us to fail to pursue the *best* that God desires for each of us beyond salvation.

> Behold I lay in Zion a choice stone, a precious corner stone, and he who believes in Him shall not be disappointed.
>
> 1 Peter 2:6 (NASB)

This truth will be very real to all who are on the new earth, and there will be much gratitude and appreciation for the gift of God each time the redeemed go and see the unbelievers who are suffering in the eternal lake of fire.

> "And it shall be from new moon to new moon And from sabbath to sabbath, All mankind will come to bow down before Me," says the Lord. "Then they shall go forth and look on the corpses of the men who have transgressed against Me. For their worm shall not die, and their fire shall not be quenched; and they shall be an abhorrence to all mankind."
>
> Isaiah 66:24 (NASB)

The new earth is going to be a place of most appreciated blessing compared to the suffering in the lake of fire. The entire human race is fallen through the sin of Adam, and none deserve to be on the new earth, and all who are there will be grateful. The eternal lake of fire is such a horrible place that God desires that none should perish in such misery.

> The Lord is not slow about His promise, as some count slowness, but is patient toward you, not wishing for any to perish but for all to come to repentance.
>
> 2 Peter 3:9 (NASB)

But those suffering eternally will be there by their own choice because they have rejected the love gift of God.

> For God so loved the world, that He gave His only begotten Son, that whoever believes in Him should not perish, but have eternal life. For God did not send the Son into the world to judge the world, but that the world should be saved through Him. He who believes in Him is not judged; he who does not believe has been judged already, because he has not believed in the name of the only begotten Son of God.
>
> John 3:16–18 (NASB)

Thanks be to God for the gift of eternal life that is freely given to all who simply receive it by faith. Also, thanks be to God that this aspect of our eternal destiny is secure in Jesus Christ and absolutely assured.

GATHERING OF THE FAITHFUL

Paul gives detail descriptions in 1 Thessalonians 4:13–18 and 1 Corinthians 15:51–53 of Jesus returning to resurrect and gather believers off the earth. The timing of this event is important in the war for dominion. Satan has been restrained from bringing forth his final evil empire until after the church, empowered by the Holy Spirit, is removed, 2 Thessalonians 2:7. After the church is removed, the powers of darkness will lead the human race into unrestrained evil, resulting in God pouring out His great wrath on the whole earth.

Paul communicated to the church in Thessalonica that they would be delivered from the coming wrath.

> For God has not destined us for wrath, but for obtaining salvation through our Lord Jesus Christ, who died for us, that whether we are awake or asleep, we may live together with Him. Therefore encourage one another, and build up one another, just as you also are doing.
>
> 1 Thessalonians 5:9–11 (NASB)

Paul writes these verses in the context of the great suffering and destruction that will come upon the earth when the day of the

Lord comes. The chapters "Three and a Half Years," "Seven Trumpets with Three Woes," and "War in Heaven" in volume 1 of this book show from the prophecies that the outpouring of God's wrath upon the earth is from the start and for the duration of the seven-year period. Therefore, the gathering of the church by Jesus Christ must take place before the seven years of wrath begins. The sequence of events written in the first few chapters of Revelation gives credence to this statement. In Revelation 2 and 3, the Apostle John records the letters from Jesus Christ to the seven churches of Asia, being the time of the church. It is no coincidence that in Revelation 4:1 John describes being taken into heaven, which has similarities to the gathering of the church in 1 Thessalonians 4:16 with the voice calling and the sound of the trumpet. John then describes the scene in the third heaven. In Revelation 5 John describes the call for someone to open the seven-seal scroll. The Lamb, Jesus Christ, comes forth and takes the scroll from the One seated on the throne, God the Father. Then all the heavenly angelic host praise and worship the Lamb.

> And they sang a new song, saying, "Worthy art Thou to take the book, and to break its seals; for Thou wast slain, and didst purchase for God with Thy blood men from every tribe and tongue and people and nation. And Thou hast made them to be a kingdom and priests to our God; and they will reign upon the earth."
>
> Revelation 5:9–10 (NASB)

The holy angelic host will sing that the Lamb is worthy to open the seven seals of the scroll because the Lamb's sacrifice has resulted in the forming "from every tribe and tongue and people and nation" of humanity a kingdom of priests who will reign upon the earth. The church is made up of people from every tribe and tongue and people and nation. The angelic host refers to these priests in their praise because just prior to this event the Lamb will have gathered His church off the earth. The faithful church is complete and standing in the third heaven when this event takes place, just as John was standing there receiving this prophecy. Immediately after the singing of praises by the heavenly host, the Lamb begins opening the seven seals of the scroll, which begins God's seven-year end-time period of wrath on the earth. Jesus Christ will gather His faithful church off the earth prior to the start of that most troublesome time of human history.

In Revelation, the Apostle John also makes mention of the Lord coming to deliver the church out of the "hour of testing," which will come upon the whole world.

> Because you have kept the word of My perseverance, I also will keep you from the hour of testing, that hour which is about to come upon the whole world, to test those who dwell upon the earth.
>
> Revelation 3:10 (NASB)

This passage reveals that the church-age believers' deliverance from the hour of testing is conditional on whether they "have kept the word of My perseverance." The Greek word translated "I also" indicates a reciprocating relationship. The Lord's action "I also will keep you from the hour of testing" has a reciprocating relationship with the action of the believers in the Philadelphia church who "kept the word of My perseverance." These words of Jesus have the implication that the inclusion of believers in the gathering will be conditional on their keeping His Word so as to persevere. No benefit is achieved, however, by ignoring or explaining away these words in this letter from Jesus Christ to the Philadelphia church. The meaning that God intends in His words will ultimately be all that matters, because God will judge according to His Word. It is much more pleasant to say that every believer from the church will be either resurrected or taken up to meet the Lord in the air at the gathering and then just move on. But this passage must be considered with other passages of God's Word about the gathering of the church to clarify this prophecy.

The most extensive writings about the gathering of the church off the earth by Jesus Christ are in Paul's letters, Philippians, 1 and 2 Thessalonians, and 1 Corinthians. Paul recounted to the church in Philippi his own efforts toward the day when Jesus resurrects and gathers His church.

> [8]More than that, I count all things to be loss in view of the surpassing value of knowing Christ Jesus my Lord, for whom I have suffered the loss of all things, and count them but rubbish in order that I may gain Christ, [9]and may be found in Him, not having a righteousness of my own derived from the Law, but that which is through faith in Christ, the righteousness which comes from God on the basis of faith, [10]that I may know Him, and the power of His resurrection and the fellowship of His sufferings, being conformed to His death; [11]in order that I may attain to the resurrection from the dead.
>
> [12]Not that I have already obtained it, or have already become perfect, but I press on in order that I may lay hold of that for which also I was laid hold of by Christ Jesus.
>
> [13]Brethren, I do not regard myself as having laid hold of it yet; but one thing I do: forgetting what lies behind and reaching forward to what lies ahead,
>
> [14]I press on toward the goal for the prize of the upward call of God in Christ Jesus.
>
> Philippians 3:8–14 (NASB)

Paul mentions the resurrection twice in this passage. The first mention is in verse 10. Just prior to this, in verses 7-9, Paul wrote about how he had surrendered all his human works of righteousness under the law and counted them as rubbish. Paul realized that all his human works of righteousness as a Pharisee were not adequate to gain the resurrection to eternal life. Only the righteousness that is given to every believer at salvation on the basis of one-time faith in Jesus Christ is adequate to enable humans to experience the "power of His resurrection" unto eternal life. At some point every believer will experience the power of God raising them from the dead. Between the first mention and the second mention of the resurrection in verse 11, Paul writes, "And the fellowship of His sufferings, being conformed to His death in order that I may attain to the resurrection from the dead." Paul uses the same Greek word for resurrection, but he adds a prefix to the word that means "out of" or "out from." The literal translation would be "that I may attain to the out from resurrection from the dead." This is referring to the resurrection that is the gathering of the faithful church off the earth. The Lord will first resurrect believers who have died, and then He will gather those who are alive "out from" the great wrath that is about to come on the earth. To obtain the "out from" resurrection Paul writes that he is endeavoring to be "conformed to His death" having "fellowship of His sufferings." The Greek word translated *attain* also means "to arrive at, to come to, to reach, to come upon." In verse 12, Paul writes, "Not that I have already obtained it, or have already become perfect." The Greek word translated *obtain* is a different word and also means "lay hold of, grasp, seize, take possession of, apprehend." Paul is communicating that in order to gain possession of the "out from" resurrection, it is necessary to have fellowship in the sufferings of Christ, and thus be conformed to His death. This resurrection is a prize that has to be obtained. There would be no need for Paul to "attain to" for the purpose of "seizing possession" of this special resurrection if it were automatically given to every church-age believer. Having the righteousness through one time faith in Jesus Christ is the first step in achieving this goal. But to seize possession believers must also forget what lies behind and reach forward to what lies ahead. This means that Paul did not live in sinless perfection. Like Paul, believers must continually confess and repent of their failures in order to move ahead unburdened by sin, Hebrews 12:1. Christians can then "press on toward the goal for the prize of the upward call of God in Christ Jesus" (verse 14). Being included in the gathering to Jesus Christ is a "prize." The meaning of the Greek word is a prize given to the victors. This is a very special and blessed and unparalleled event in human history. It is not reasonable that it would be given to just any believers. Thankfully, the Lord does not require believers to achieve sinless perfection in this temporal life to attain the honor of this exclusive resurrection. What is required to attain the prize is that believers persistently endeavor to become more like Christ. The way that we press on toward the goal is by being conformed to the likeness of Jesus in His death by daily sacrificing the flesh nature with its lusts, Romans 8:13. Believers must persistently lay aside the old self and become transformed by the Word of God through the power of the Holy Spirit, Ephesians 4:22–24. Every believer of every age of human history will ultimately experience the power of the resurrection. But only faithful believers will "attain" the first resurrection of the redeemed and be gathered to meet the Lord in the air. At the time that Paul wrote his letter to the Philippians, he indicated that he had not yet attained the prize of this first and privileged resurrection. Paul was not implying, however, that he had not been faithful enough. Earlier in the letter, Paul wrote he was confident that if he were to be face-to-face with the Lord at that time, it would be gain for him.

> For to me, to live is Christ, and to die is gain. But if I am to live on in the flesh, this will mean fruitful labor for me; and I do not know which to choose. But I am hard-pressed from both directions, having the desire to depart and be with Christ, for that is very much better; yet to remain on in the flesh is more necessary for your sake.
>
> Philippians 1:21–24 (NASB)

Paul was confident that Jesus Christ counted him faithful at the time he wrote this; however, Paul knew that it was not yet time for him to die because the Lord had more work for him to accomplish.

The Apostle Paul had a very obvious urgency in his letters about the coming of the Lord because he believed it could happen even in His lifetime. When Paul wrote about the Lord gathering off the earth those who are still alive, he always included himself.

> Then we who are alive and remain shall be caught up together with them in the clouds to meet the Lord in the air.
>
> 1 Thessalonians 5:17 (NASB)

> Behold, I tell you a mystery; we shall not all sleep, but we shall all be changed.
>
> 1 Corinthians 15:51 (NASB)

Acts 1:6–11 documents the ascension of the Lord Jesus Christ back to the third heaven. After Jesus disappeared from sight in the clouds, the disciples kept looking up to see if He was returning immediately. The angels appeared and reassured them that Jesus would return. The coming of Christ to gather His faithful church has been imminent since the day Jesus ascended. God has intentionally concealed the exact time this event will take place, as Jesus told the disciples before He ascended.

> He said to them, "It is not for you to know times or epochs which the Father has fixed by His own authority."
>
> Acts 1:7 (NASB)

God has not revealed the time that Jesus will return for His faithful church because God wants it to be a motivator for believers throughout the time of the church to always be ready.

In his letters to believers in the early churches, the Apostle Paul repeatedly and exigently communicated that they must be vigilant in living obedient lives in anticipation of the Lord's return.

> And this I pray, that your love may abound still more and more in real knowledge and all discernment, so that you may approve the things that are excellent, in order to be sincere and blameless until the day of Christ.
>
> Philippians 1:9–10 (NASB)

Paul prayed for the believers in Philippi that they have knowledge that will cause their love to abound. Paul prayed this because there was a potential that those believers would fail to achieve this abundant love. If they failed, then they would not be found to be sincere and blameless when Christ returns to gather from the earth those who are the faithful. Even though Paul did not specify any consequences if they failed, he thought it crucial enough to pray for the believers in Philippi to succeed. Later in the Philippians letter, Paul again expresses his concern about the status of these believers in the coming day of the Lord.

> So then, my beloved, just as you have always obeyed, not as in my presence only, but now much more in my absence, work out your salvation with fear and trembling.
>
> Philippians 2:12 (NASB)

> That you may prove yourselves to be blameless and innocent, children of God above reproach in the midst of a crooked and perverse generation, among whom you appear as lights in the world, holding fast the word of life, so that in the day of Christ I may have cause to glory because I did not run in vain nor toil in vain.
>
> Philippians 2:15–16 (NASB)

Paul warns the church to "work out your salvation with fear and trembling." This indicates serious consequence for failure to do so. The consequence is not loss of salvation, but loss that is associated with the "day of Christ" when He returns to gather His faithful church. Here again Paul reveals the means that God has provided for our compliance, "holding fast the Word of life." Believers who fail to persistently pursue God through His Word will fail, and they will miss out on the day of Christ. Paul warns of the destiny of those distracted, unfaithful, and neglectful children of God.

> For many walk, of whom I often told you, and now tell you even weeping, that they are enemies of the cross of Christ, whose end is destruction, whose god is their appetite, and whose glory is in their shame, who set their minds on earthly things. For our citizenship is in heaven, from which also we eagerly wait for a Savior, the Lord Jesus Christ; who will transform the body of our humble state into conformity with the body of His glory, by the exertion of the power that He has even to subject all things to Himself.
>
> Philippians 3:18–21 (NASB)

Paul wept as he wrote about these individuals because they were fellow believers who had become distracted by the temptations of this temporal world so that they reverted to indulging in the lusts of their flesh natures. They were "enemies of the cross" in that their lives were a negative witness of the gift of salvation that was freely given to them. They looked like the world and could not be distinguished from the world. The Greek word translated *destruction* also means "consumption, waste, profusion, ruin." Their "end is destruction" has both temporal and eternal connotation. In the temporal, it means they will suffer the punishment by premature physical death, 1 Corinthians 11:30–32 and 1 John

5:16–17. The disgrace of punishment by physical death will be compounded at the judgment seat of Jesus Christ by the loss of eternal rewards. Believers who set their minds on earthly things are distracted and have no regard for the return of the Savior. Only those who are focused on their heavenly citizenship will eagerly watch for the return of Jesus Christ. At His coming, the Savior will transform the bodies of those who "eagerly wait" into bodies like His own, Philippians 3:21. Believers who are enemies of the cross will not receive this blessed reward from the Savior because He is not going to take them with Him. Paul wept for those believers, but they will weep for themselves at the time of their judgment. Looking for the blessed hope has been the motivator that God has given to every believer throughout the time of the church.

> For the grace of God has appeared, bringing salvation to all men, instructing us to deny ungodliness and worldly desires and to live sensibly, righteously and godly in the present age, looking for the blessed hope and the appearing of the glory of our great God and Savior, Christ Jesus; who gave Himself for us, that He might redeem us from every lawless deed and purify for Himself a people for His own possession, zealous for good deeds.
>
> Titus 2:11–14 (NASB)

The Greek word translated *hope* means "having assured expectation." The "blessed hope" of believers is their confidence in the appearing of Jesus Christ. The Savior gave Himself as a sacrifice so He could "purify for Himself a people for His own possession, zealous for good deeds." Believers who fail to "deny ungodliness and worldly desires" are failing to be purified. Unfaithful believers hope only for the fulfillment of their lustful desires in the world. Believers who take seriously the warnings and consequences about the return of Jesus Christ are like students who have prepared for an exam and look forward to it with confidence. Believers who are prepared are eager for the Lord to come and take them off this corrupt earth, therefore they love His appearing.

> And inasmuch as it is appointed for men to die once and after this comes judgment, so Christ also, having been offered once to bear the sins of many, shall appear a second time for salvation without reference to sin, to those who eagerly await Him.
>
> Hebrews 9:27–28 (NASB)

The salvation referred to in this passage is deliverance from the end time of tribulation on the earth. When Jesus Christ returns to gather those who will be delivered, He will appear face-to-face only "to those who eagerly await Him."

> In the future there is laid up for me the crown of righteousness, which the Lord, the righteous Judge, will award to me on that day; and not only to me, but also to all who have loved His appearing.
>
> 2 Timothy 4:8 (NASB)

The Apostle Paul reveals that the Lord will give this reward to "all who have loved His appearing." Believers who have no urgency and no regard for the return of Jesus Christ will not receive this reward. Crowns are for those who will reign with Christ. Jesus Christ will gather only the faithful believers who will be given the reward of reigning with Him. This will be the dominion of the faithful. So those who lack the reward of the crown will also lack the reward of being included in the gathering of the faithful church. God has supplied every believer all that is needed in this temporal life to achieve the rewards.

> That in everything you were enriched in Him, in all speech
> and all knowledge, even as the testimony concerning
> Christ was confirmed in you, so that you are not lacking in
> any gift, awaiting eagerly the revelation of our Lord Jesus
> Christ, who shall also confirm you to the end, blameless in
> the day of our Lord Jesus Christ.
>
> 1 Corinthians 1:5–8 (NASB)

The Corinth church had many spiritual assets from God. Sadly, the many wonderful gifts became a source of arrogance and competition, for which Paul rebuked them. The Corinth believers understood and looked eagerly for the return of the Lord Jesus Christ; however, that truth also became a source of arrogance to them.

> For who regards you as superior? And what do you have
> that you did not receive? But if you did receive it, why do
> you boast as if you had not received it? You are already
> filled, you have already become rich, you have become
> kings without us; and I would indeed that you had become
> kings so that we also might reign with you.
>
> 1 Corinthians 4:7–8 (NASB)

Some of the believers in Corinth were boasting about the spiritual gifts they had received and thought themselves superior. It was as though they thought they had acquired the miraculous abilities associated with the gifts on their own. In conjunction, they also assumed that their superior ability meant they had already arrived and were certainly destined to reign as kings with Christ. Paul sarcastically writes, "You are already filled, you have already become rich, you have become kings without us" (1 Corinthains 4:8). Even though the Corinth church had many internal problems, yet they took seriously the promise of the return of Jesus Christ and the promise of reigning with Him. When Paul was in Corinth, he taught this truth to them, desiring to engrain it in their minds. The return of Jesus Christ was an urgent and crucial matter to the Apostle Paul because he knew there will be serious and immediate consequences on that day. If the coming of Jesus Christ at any moment was so weighty to Paul in the early church, then it certainly ought to be urgent to every believer in the church now.

The early church that Paul most commended for living in this reality was the church in Thessalonica. In the first letter Paul sent to the Thessalonians he gave the church a glowing review.

> [2]We give thanks to God always for all of you, making mention of you in our prayers; [3]constantly bearing in mind your work of faith and labor of love and steadfastness of hope in our Lord Jesus Christ in the presence of our God and Father, [4]knowing, brethren beloved by God, His choice of you; [5]for our gospel did not come to you in word only, but also in power and in the Holy Spirit and with full conviction; just as you know what kind of men we proved to be among you for your sake.
>
> [6]You also became imitators of us and of the Lord, having received the word in much tribulation with the joy of the Holy Spirit, [7]so that you became an example to all the believers in Macedonia and in Achaia.
>
> [8]For the word of the Lord has sounded forth from you, not only in Macedonia and Achaia, but also in every place your faith toward God has gone forth, so that we have no need to say anything.
>
> [9]For they themselves report about us what kind of a reception we had with you, and how you turned to God from idols to serve a living and true God, [10]and to wait for His Son from heaven, whom He raised from the dead, that is Jesus, who delivers us from the wrath to come.
>
> 1 Thessalonians 1:2–10 (NASB)

The period of time that Paul called "the wrath to come" is the same as "the hour of testing, that hour which is about to come upon the whole world" that John wrote about in Revelation in 3:10. Paul commended the church in Thessalonica because their waiting for the Son to come from heaven to deliver them from the wrath motivated them to turn away from idols to serve the true God. In verse 3, Paul gives this church accolades for their work of faith, labor of love, and steadfast hope. In verse 6, Paul says they have become imitators of him and the Lord. They had received the word joyfully through tribulation. This church was well on its way toward the goal of being delivered from the coming wrath, verse 10.

In 1 Thessalonians 4, Paul continues the teaching on the subject of being delivered from the wrath by assuring them that the dead in Christ shall rise first and then those who are alive will also be caught up to meet the Lord in the air.

> [13]But we do not want you to be uninformed, brethren, about those who are asleep, that you may not grieve, as do the rest who have no hope.
>
> [14]For if we believe that Jesus died and rose again, even so God will bring with Him those who have fallen asleep in Jesus.
>
> [15]For this we say to you by the word of the Lord, that we who are alive, and remain until the coming of the Lord, shall not precede those who have fallen asleep.
>
> [16]For the Lord Himself will descend from heaven with a shout, with the voice of the archangel, and with the trumpet of God; and the dead in Christ shall rise first.
>
> [17]Then we who are alive and remain shall be caught up together with them in the clouds to meet the Lord in the air, and thus we shall always be with the Lord.
>
> [18]Therefore comfort one another with these words.
>
> 1 Thessalonians 4:13–18 (NASB)

In verse 13, Paul reminds the believers in Thessalonica that they have a hope, so there is no need for them to grieve over fellow believers who have died. As in Titus 2:13 and 1 Thessalonians 1:3, Paul again uses the word *hope* when writing about the return of Jesus Christ to gather His faithful church off the earth. Believers who have a confident expectation of this event are living in the reality of the blessed hope. They have a peaceful sense about physical death so it is no more fearful than having "fallen asleep." There are Christians who do not believe this prophecy or have doubts about it. These believers mourn and grieve over physical death, and they fear death the same as unbelievers. To them, physical death is not as unobtrusive as falling asleep. Believers who reject the promise of being gathered to Christ or who have neglected this blessed hope are the exact opposite of the believers Paul is addressing in 1 Thessalonians 4:13. In verse 14, Paul assures the faithful believers in Thessalonica that their fellow Christians who had fallen asleep will be included in the gathering to Christ. Paul exhorts them that as they are confident in their own salvation so also they can be completely confident that the Lord will bring with Him those of the Thessalonica church who are asleep. Verse 14 can be worded, "Since you believe that Jesus died and rose again, in the same way believe that God will bring with Him those who have slept through Jesus." The translation "slept through Jesus" is more accurate to the original Greek text. The word Paul uses often indicates more than just being in a position, "in Jesus." Paul uses this word in Philippians 4:13: "I can do all things through Him who strengthens me" (NASB). The implication is that there is an effort put forth by the believer to accomplish a goal through Jesus Christ. Those "who have fallen asleep through Jesus" have put forth an effort to achieve this status. Paul refers to their death as having "fallen asleep" because they are resting from their efforts and works "through Christ." These believers are also those who have been purified because they lived in anticipation of the Lord's appearing. When Jesus Christ comes to gather the faithful, He will bring with Him those who are resting from their works. Conversely, Jesus Christ will not bring with Him believers who have died producing works of the flesh. This shows that the conditional gathering prophecy written by John in Revelation 3:10 fits with this prophetic passage about the gathering written by Paul. The prophecy written by John is just clearer and more concise. At the end of verse 16 in 1 Thessalonians 4, Paul wrote the phrase "the dead in Christ shall rise first." Paul uses a different Greek word translated *in* for the phrase "dead in Christ." This correlates with what Paul writes in Romans 6 about believers being untied with Christ in His death.

> [3]Or do you not know that all of us who have been baptized into Christ Jesus have been baptized into His death?
>
> [4]Therefore we have been buried with Him through baptism into death, so that as Christ was raised from the dead through the glory of the Father, so we too might walk in newness of life.
>
> [5]For if we have become united with Him in the likeness of His death, certainly we shall also be in the likeness of His resurrection, [6]knowing this, that our old self was crucified with Him, in order that our body of sin might be done away with, so that we would no longer be slaves to sin; [7]for he who has died is freed from sin.
>
> [11]Even so consider yourselves to be dead to sin, but alive to God in Christ Jesus.
>
> [12]Therefore do not let sin reign in your mortal body so that you obey its lusts,
>
> [16]Do you not know that when you present yourselves to someone *as* slaves for obedience, you are slaves of the one whom you obey, either of sin resulting in death, or of obedience resulting in righteousness?
>
> Romans 6:3–7, 11–12, and 16 (NASB)

In verses 3 and 4, Paul states the reality that all who believe the gospel of Jesus Christ are baptized with Him in His death. At the end of verse 4, Paul writes that this sets up the possibility that believers "might walk in newness of life." This is contingent on each believer's choices, so it is not always a reality in a believer's life. In verse 6, Paul reveals that every believer's "old self" is what was crucified on the cross with Christ, with the result that believers might be free from sin. This again is contingent on each believer's choices and not always a reality in a believer's life. Every believer can be free so not to walk in sin. In verse 12, Paul mandates believers to not live in the lusts of their flesh. Paul issues a warning in verse 16 that disobedience will result in death. This is not eternal death in the lake of fire, but rather suffering physical death as God's discipline and the loss of eternal rewards. To summarize, every believer has the position of being dead in Christ at the point of salvation. Believers who take advantage of the crucifixion of their old self will have the experiential condition of being dead in Christ while still in this temporal life. In verse 5, Paul writes that every believer will most certainly be resurrected from the dead as Jesus was resurrected; however, this does not mean every believer will be included in the gathering to Christ. In Romans 8 Paul reveals the means that God has provided for believers to achieve the experiential condition of being dead in Christ.

> So then, brethren, we are under obligation, not to the flesh, to live according to the flesh for if you are living according to the flesh, you must die; but if by the Spirit you are putting to death the deeds of the body, you will live.
>
> Romans 8:12–13 (NASB)

The Holy Spirit residing in each believer is the only One who can continually put to death the flesh nature, Galatians 5:16–21. The daily experiential crucifixion of the flesh nature is by the power of the Holy Spirit. Walking in the Spirit and being experientially dead in Christ are one in the same.

> Now those who belong to Christ Jesus have crucified the flesh with its passions and desires. If we live by the Spirit, let us also walk by the Spirit.
>
> Galatians 5:24–25 (NASB)

All believers are the eternal possession of Jesus Christ, but only those who crucify their flesh natures "belong to Christ" in the context of this passage. These are the ones who will have the inheritance rewards of the kingdom that Paul referred to earlier in this passage, Galatians 5:21. Jesus communicated this same truth to his disciples.

> And He was saying to them all, "If anyone wishes to come after Me, he must deny himself, and take up his cross daily and follow Me. "For whoever wishes to save his life will lose it, but whoever loses his life for My sake, he is the one who will save it. "For what is a man profited if he gains the whole world, and loses or forfeits himself?
>
> Luke 9:23–25 (NASB)

> And he who does not take his cross and follow after Me is not worthy of Me.
>
> Matthew 10:38 (NASB)

Taking up the cross and following Jesus is the daily crucifixion of the flesh nature. Jesus is not saying this is the means to salvation from the eternal lake of fire. Rather, Jesus is saying this is the means of avoiding loss of the abundant eternal life of rewards, 2 Peter 1:6–11. Matthew records that Jesus said those who fail to crucify their flesh are not worthy of Him, meaning worthy of His inheritance. Believers who fail to crucify their flesh natures daily will put the pursuit of their fleshly lusts and the things of this temporal world as their first priority. Those believers will forfeit and lose the life of eternal reward blessings. One of the rewards they forfeit is being gathered with other faithful believers off the earth when Jesus returns for His faithful church.

Going back to 1 Thessalonians 4:16, Paul writes, "The dead in Christ shall rise first." This refers to those who have both the position of being dead in Christ and the experiential condition of being dead in Christ. Deceased believers who lived considering themselves dead to sin so that they walked in the newness of life are the "dead in Christ." Believers who continually resuscitate their flesh nature so that they walk in death are experientially the dead in the flesh, not the dead in Christ. Believers who continually walk in the fleshly death will be excluded from the special resurrection that will happen at the gathering to Christ. All believers go to be present with the Lord at physical death, 2 Corinthians 5:8, but the Lord will bring only the faithful with Him for this special resurrection. Next, in verse 17, Paul describes the most amazing event that believers throughout the church age have anticipated experiencing, which is being caught up to meet the Lord in the air while still alive on this earth. As seen in other passages, the promise of this unique blessing has motivated believers since the time of the early church to live in obedience to Jesus Christ. The promise of this event gives both hope and comfort, as Paul directs believers to "comfort one another with these words" in 1 Thessalonians 4:8.

This assurance and comfort is not needed solely for overcoming the fear of physical death. Paul communicated this information to the church in Thessalonica to give them confidence that they would be delivered out of the unprecedented suffering of the prophesied end times.

¹But concerning the times and the seasons, brethren, you have no need that I should write to you.

²For you yourselves know perfectly that the day of the Lord so comes as a thief in the night.

³For when they say, "Peace and safety!" then sudden destruction comes upon them, as labor pains upon a pregnant woman. And they shall not escape.

⁴But you, brethren, are not in darkness, so that this Day should overtake you as a thief.

⁵You are all sons of light and sons of the day. We are not of the night nor of darkness.

⁶Therefore let us not sleep, as others do, but let us watch and be sober.

⁷For those who sleep, sleep at night, and those who get drunk are drunk at night.

⁸But let us who are of the day be sober, putting on the breastplate of faith and love, and as a helmet the hope of salvation.

¹⁰For God did not appoint us to wrath, but to obtain salvation through our Lord Jesus Christ, who died for us, that whether we wake or sleep, we should live together with Him.

¹¹Therefore comfort each other and edify one another, just as you also are doing.

1 Thessalonians 5:1–11 (NKJV)

From verse 1 and 2, Paul is writing these things to these believers as a refresher course of what he had taught them regarding the coming wrath of the day of the Lord. The suffering that the Lord will bring upon those alive on the earth will be like a woman's birth pangs. As seen in volume one, the plagues that the Lord will bring upon the earth throughout the seven-year period will be very fearful. The gathering of the faithful church by Jesus Christ must take place prior to the start of the day of the Lord, which is not a single day when the Lord comes but includes the whole seven-year period of Daniel's seventieth week. In verse 4, Paul tells the church in Thessalonica that they should not be overtaken by the day of the Lord. The reason they should not be overtaken is because they are sons of light who should be caught up to meet the Lord in the air, as Paul wrote in the verses just previous to this. In verses 5 through 7, Paul reminds believers that they are "sons of light and sons of day." Those who are "of the night" are unbelievers. Paul commands that the sons of light are not to "sleep" or "get drunk" like those who are of the night. Believers can and do live as those who are of the night. If believers automatically lived as sons of light, then there would be no need for Paul to give this command. This passage by Paul correlates very well the warning the Apostle John wrote about believers walking in darkness.

> This is the message which we have heard from Him and declare to you, that God is light and in Him is no darkness at all. If we say that we have fellowship with Him, and walk in darkness, we lie and do not practice the truth.
>
> 1 John 1:5–6 (NASB)

The home of every believer in Jesus Christ is in the light; we are not of the night or the darkness. But sons of light can wander away from home into the darkness if they are not continuously vigilant in their walk. In verse 8, Paul directs that believers who want to be "alert and sober" have to "put on the breastplate of faith and love, and as a helmet, the hope of salvation." This is a parallel passage to Ephesians 6:10–20, which is about believers living in regard of the spiritual warfare, which is a crucial part of believers being delivered out of the wrath coming on the earth. Continuing in verse 9, Paul writes, "For God has not destined us for wrath, but for obtaining salvation through our Lord Jesus Christ." Paul is presenting believers a decision that they must make. We can either live as sons of light so as to obtain salvation, or we can live as those who are of the night and be destined for the wrath. This is not referring to the eternal salvation from the eternal lake of fire, which is received as a gift through a one-time faith in Jesus Christ. In this passage, Paul is referring to salvation from the severe suffering that will result from the wrath that will come with the day of the Lord. This salvation has to be *obtained*. In Philippians 3:11–12, Paul wrote about obtaining the out-from resurrection, which is the gathering to Jesus Christ. The Greek word Paul uses in 1 Thessalonians 5:19 that is translated *obtaining* is a different word than the word he used in Philippians 3:12, but the two words are very close in meaning. The Greek word used in this passage means "lay up, acquire, obtain, acquisition." Believers who fail to live as sons of the light and of the day will not obtain the salvation from wrath that will come with day of the Lord. They will be left on the earth. In verse 11, Paul commands believers, "Therefore comfort each other and edify one another, just as you also are doing." This is the second time in this passage that Paul commands believers to comfort one another with the prophecy of the gathering to the Lord. The Greek word translated *comfort* is the same word Paul used in 1 Thessalonians 4:18. But in repeating this command, Paul adds that this prophecy is also to be used to "edify" other believers. The Greek word translated *comfort* can also mean "encourage, persuade, exhort, beseech, implore, entreat." The Greek word translated *edify* can also mean "to establish, to contribute to advancement." Believers are to use the serious and sobering realities of the prophecy about the gathering to Christ and the day of the Lord to exhort and implore other believers in order to help them to stand firm in their obedience. Both places where the Greek is translated *comfort* in this passage, it is likely that Paul also intended the dynamic meaning of "persuade and exhort and implore," considering the context of this passage. At the beginning of this letter, 1 Thessalonians 1:9–10, Paul commends the believers in that church for heeding his warnings about the return of the Son of God from heaven. Paul expresses urgency about this event throughout this letter, and at the end, he offers a fervent prayer for them regarding coming of the Jesus Christ.

> But examine everything carefully; hold fast to that which is good; abstain from every form of evil. Now may the God of peace Himself sanctify you entirely; and may your spirit and soul and body be preserved complete, without blame at the coming of our Lord Jesus Christ. Faithful is He who calls you, and He also will bring it to pass.
>
> 1 Thessalonians 5:21–24 (NASB)

Paul lived his life and taught the churches as though the coming of Jesus Christ was going to happen in his lifetime. Paul exhorts the church to carefully examine everything, which enables believers to discern if something is good so as to hold fast to it, or to determine it is evil so as to abstain from it. "Examine everything carefully" refers to the condition inside our hearts as well as things outside. Believers must be vigilant to scrutinize every aspect of their own lives with a spiritual eye. There must be a continuous judging of oneself to avoid being a partaker of the darkness, and a diligence in getting back into the light when fallen from living as a son of light. If believers fail to heed Paul's warning, then there is great risk that they will not be found blameless when the Lord comes, and there will be a serious consequence. Considering the solemn nature of this event, believers need to be diligent in offering up this same prayer for fellow believers. Only God can enable a believer to be found blameless at the coming of the Lord. But God will accomplish this only for believers who are holding fast to good and abstaining from every form of evil.

The gathering of the faithful church by Jesus Christ is the catalyst that begins the day of the Lord. Between the writing of 1

Thessalonians and 2 Thessalonians a false teaching had come into that church, saying that the day of the Lord had already begun.

> Now we request you, brethren, with regard to the coming of our Lord Jesus Christ, and our gathering together to Him, that you may not be quickly shaken from your composure or be disturbed either by a spirit or a message or a letter as if from us, to the effect that the day of the Lord has come.
>
> 2 Thessalonians 2:1–2 (NASB)

The truth that Paul had told these believers in the first letter, to comfort and exhort them to obedience, had come under attack by a lie that the day of Lord had started, which means the gathering of the church had already happened. Those spreading the lie were seeking to exploit this truth so as to discourage this church that was having such a great impact. The lie was especially despicable because in reality this was one of the most faithful churches of that time, as revealed by Paul at the beginning of his first letter to the church in Thessalonica. It is no wonder that the enemy wanted to put this church in turmoil with the lie because their reputation and their outreach had extended throughout the region, 1 Thessalonians 1:7–8. The motivation of these believers in being a witness and an example was their waiting for God's Son from heaven to come and deliver them out of the wrath to come, 1 Thessalonians 1:9–10. Paul had told them in the first letter that they were doing everything right. Sometime after that, they were exposed to false teaching that cast doubt on whether they were conducting themselves in a way that was pleasing to God. For this reason, Paul begins the second letter to the Thessalonians again assuring them they were pleasing to God.

> We ought always to give thanks to God for you, brethren, as is only fitting, because your faith is greatly enlarged, and the love of each one of you toward one another grows

ever greater; therefore, we ourselves speak proudly of you among the churches of God for your perseverance and faith in the midst of all your persecutions and afflictions which you endure. This is a plain indication of God's righteous judgment so that you may be considered worthy of the kingdom of God, for which indeed you are suffering.

2 Thessalonians 1:3–5 (NASB)

In verse 5, Paul tells them they are "considered worthy of the kingdom of God," meaning they were going to be included in the gathering to Christ. Believers who are worthy of the kingdom are also worthy to obtain the resurrection at the gathering to Christ. After reassuring the believers in Thessalonica that they are pleasing to God, Paul proceeds with countering the destructive lie that had caused them such turmoil.

Now we request you, brethren, with regard to the coming of our Lord Jesus Christ, and our gathering together to Him, that you may not be quickly shaken from your composure or be disturbed either by a spirit or a message or a letter as if from us, to the effect that the day of the Lord has come. Let no one in any way deceive you, for it will not come unless the apostasy comes first, and the man of lawlessness is revealed, the son of destruction, who opposes and exalts himself above every so-called god or object of worship, so that he takes his seat in the temple of God, displaying himself as being God. Do you not remember that while I was still with you, I was telling you these things?

2 Thessalonians 2:1–5 (NASB)

The believers in Thessalonica were "quickly shaken," thinking they had not been included in the "gathering together to Him." If Paul had taught them that every member of the body of Christ would be taken at the gathering, whether obedient or disobedient, then it would have been simple for the Thessalonica church to refute and reject the lie that the day of the Lord had already come. But if Paul had taught them that the gathering to Christ is conditional on obedience, then there was a potential that they could be excluded. Thus, these believers were "quickly shaken" from their composure, thinking they had not been found worthy. Paul reminds them of some indicators they can look for to determine whether the day of the Lord has begun. Notice that Paul doesn't include as an indicator, "if you're still on the earth then the day of the Lord has not yet come." Logically that should have been the first indicator he would have listed if the entire church is gathered by Christ. Instead, Paul reminds them that if they see the apostasy or a falling away from God occur, then they can be sure that they missed the gathering of the faithful church by Jesus Christ. The removal of the faithful church will be a catalyst for the falling away by the human inhabitants left on the earth. To counter the lies that had disturbed these believers, in 2 Thessalonians 2:1–3 Paul clearly gives the sequence of the events that must take place. First, the restrainer has to be taken out of the way. Second, the falling away will come and the man of lawlessness will be revealed. Third, the day of the Lord will come. Paul reminds them that the day of the Lord begins after the revealing of the man of lawlessness. Then Paul reiterates his previous teaching to them that the man of lawlessness cannot be revealed till the restrainer is taken out of the way.

> And you know what restrains him now, so that in his time he may be revealed. For the mystery of lawlessness is already at work; only he who now restrains will do so until he is taken out of the way. And then that lawless one will be revealed whom the Lord will slay with the breath of His mouth and bring to an end by the appearance of His coming; that is, the one whose coming is in accord with the activity of Satan, with all power and signs and false wonders.
>
> 2 Thessalonians 2:6–9 (NASB)

The identity of the restrainer is given in the context of the letter. The only thing mentioned as being taken away is the church at the gathering to Jesus Christ in verse 1. The restrainer is the church empowered by the Holy Spirit. Only the Holy Spirit is able to empower the church for this mighty task. In this age, God has made the church to have a very powerful role in the war for dominion. At the time the church was formed, the head of the scarlet beast representing Rome was in power, Revelation 17:9–10. No more heads of the scarlet beast have been raised up since the formation of the church. But that is not because Satan has given up. In verse, 7 Paul writes that the effort to raise up a lawless one continues even while the restrainer is still in place, but it has been unsuccessful.

> And every spirit that does not confess Jesus is not from God; and this is the spirit of the antichrist, of which you have heard that it is coming, and now it is already in the world. You are from God, little children, and have overcome them; because greater is He who is in you than he who is in the world.
>
> 1 John 4:3–4 (NASB)

The church has overcome the spirit of the Antichrist by the power of the Holy Spirit living in them.

In 2 Thessalonians 2, Paul makes two references to the coming of Jesus Christ.

> Now we request you, brethren, with regard to the coming of our Lord Jesus Christ, and our gathering together to Him
>
> 2 Thessalonians 2:1 (NASB)

> And then that lawless one will be revealed whom the Lord will slay with the breath of His mouth and bring to an end by the appearance of His coming
>
> 2 Thessalonians 2:8 (NASB)

These cannot be the same coming or appearing. The first is before the apostasy begins and the second is after the apostasy begins. So the day that Jesus Christ comes to gather the faithful church is not the same day that He comes to slay the lawless one. These are two very different events with two very different purposes.

The man of lawlessness, 2 Thessalonians 2:3 and 8, is the same individual the prophet Daniel calls "the prince of the people."

> Then after the sixty-two weeks the Messiah will be cut off and have nothing, and the people of the prince who is to come will destroy the city and the sanctuary...
>
> And he will make a firm covenant with the many for one week, but in the middle of the week he will put a stop to sacrifice and grain offering; and on the wing of abominations will come one who makes desolate, even until a complete destruction, one that is decreed, is poured out on the one who makes desolate.
>
> Daniel 9:26–27 (NASB)

The revealing of the man of lawlessness begins at the making of the firm covenant, which is at the start of the seven-year period. The revealing of the lawless one and the Day of the Lord cannot begin until the faithful church is removed. Anyone left on the earth when the covenant is confirmed can be sure they have been excluded from the gathering to Christ. The gradual unveiling of the man of lawlessness will occur during the first three and a half years. At the middle of the seven years, he will be fully revealed in all his wickedness at the abomination that brings desolation.

In 2 Thessalonians 2:5, Paul states that what he was writing was a reminder of things he had told them previously. When Paul was present in Thessalonica, he must have taught them about a conditional gathering, so they were aware that exclusion meant they had failed in walking with the Lord. Being included is conditional on perseverance. The term *conditional gathering* is preferred over the term *partial gathering*. The latter gives the idea that believers will be gathered in stage, meaning part of the body of Christ will be taken at one point and the rest will be taken at a later point. But there is only one gathering of the faithful members out the body of Christ and off the earth. This is a once-in-eternity opportunity, and those who are excluded will have missed it forever.

Paul uses to the word *mystery* when teaching the believers in Corinth about the resurrection of the dead at the gathering to Jesus Christ.

> Behold, I tell you a mystery; we shall not all sleep, but we shall all be changed, in a moment, in the twinkling of an eye, at the last trumpet; for the trumpet will sound, and the dead will be raised imperishable, and we shall be changed.
>
> 1 Corinthians 15:51–52 (NASB)

Paul also referred to the sounding of the trumpet when writing about this event in his first letter to the church at Thessalonica.

> For the Lord Himself will descend from heaven with a shout, with the voice of the archangel, and with the trumpet of God; and the dead in Christ shall rise first.
>
> 1 Thessalonians 4:16 (NASB)

The "last trumpet" is not related to the seven trumpet plagues of Revelation. Paul wrote these letters to the churches at Thessalonica and Corinth early in the church age, long before the Revelation was written by John. The churches had no knowledge of the trumpet plagues so they would not have associated the "last trumpet" with the trumpet plagues. Instead, there will be two soundings of the trumpet for the glorious gathering of the faithful church off the earth. With the first trumpet sound, the dead in Christ will arise. With the second or last trumpet, those who are still alive will be caught up and instantly changed to being imperishable.

In 1 Corinthians 15:51, Paul writes, "We shall not *all* sleep, but we shall *all* be changed" (NASB, emphasis mine). If "all" refers to the whole body of Christ, then the gathering to Christ is unconditional and no believer will be excluded. It can be determined from the context of this passage whether Paul is including all the church. Paul wrote this letter to the Corinthian church because they had many sin problems. These were not believers walking in obedience by the power of the Holy Spirit. One of the many problems facing this church included a group of believers who did not believe in the resurrection, and were even mocking the teaching.

> Now if Christ is preached, that He has been raised from the dead, how do some among you say that there is no resurrection of the dead?
>
> 1 Corinthians 15:12 (NASB)

> But someone will say, "How are the dead raised? And with what kind of body do they come?" You fool! That which you sow does not come to life unless it dies.
>
> 1 Corinthians 15:35–36 (NASB)

In 1 Corinthians 15, Paul is countering the mockers who were saying that there is no resurrection. The entire chapter teaches the importance of the resurrection from the dead as our great hope. This was the same satanic lie that Jesus encountered with the Sadducees, Luke 20:27. In Corinth, this heresy had not come from outside the church but had developed from within. To relieve any doubt or division that the naysayers had caused, the Corinthian church needed the reassuring words from Paul about the transformation of believers who had died and whose bodies were in the grave. Paul took the opportunity, however, to use this teaching to admonish the Corinthian church to walk with the Lord. When Paul writes to them, "we shall not all sleep," he is reminding them of the reward of being found worthy to be taken by Christ when He gathers His faithful church. Paul begins this section of the letter by telling the Corinth believers that they must "hold fast the word."

> ¹Now I make known to you, brethren, the gospel which I preached to you, which also you received, in which also you stand, ²by which also you are saved, if you hold fast the word which I preached to you, unless you believed in vain.
> ³For I delivered to you as of first importance what I also received, that Christ died for our sins according to the Scriptures, ⁴and that He was buried, and that He was raised on the third day according to the Scriptures.
>
> 1 Corinthians 15:1–4 (NASB)

Paul returns to very elementary truth to walk these believers through the problem they had with the resurrection. They had already received this whole gospel, which means they accepted it as truth. Having done this, they were saved. The gospel includes the truth that Jesus was raised on the third day. Those who were later rejecting the teaching of the resurrection were failing to "hold fast the word" in its entirety. As a result, that truth no longer had any benefit to them because they lost the assurance that the resurrection brings to believers. The English translation of this verse seems to indicate that being saved is conditional upon holding fast the word. In the Greek text, verse 2 literally reads, "Through which you were saved, to what word I preached to you if you hold fast except unless in vain you believed." Holding fast has nothing to do with being saved, but it does affect whether the word preached continues to be beneficial. A believer who doubts the resurrection will lose hope and will have no motivation to live a godly life. Paul describes the attitude of vanity that results in the hearts of believers who reject the truth of the resurrection.

> And if Christ has not been raised, then our preaching is vain, your faith also is vain... and if Christ has not been raised, your faith is worthless; you are still in your sins.
>
> 1 Corinthians 15:14 and 17 (NASB)

> If from human motives I fought with wild beasts at Ephesus, what does it profit me? If the dead are not raised, let us eat and drink, for tomorrow we die. Do not be deceived: "Bad company corrupts good morals." Become sober-minded as you ought, and stop sinning; for some have no knowledge of God. I speak this to your shame.
>
> 1 Corinthians 15:32–34 (NASB)

Those believers in Corinth who had rejected the teaching of the resurrection were in danger of being excluded from the eternal rewards that come after the resurrection. Even worse, they were leading others down the same vain path. Paul reinforces the truth of the resurrection to renew the assurance of those who were still holding fast the word.

> For this perishable must put on the imperishable, and this mortal must put on immortality. But when this perishable will have put on the imperishable, and this mortal will have put on immortality, then will come about the saying that is written, "Death is swallowed up in victory. "O death, where is your victory? O death, where is your sting?" The sting of death is sin, and the power of sin is the law; but thanks be to God, who gives us the victory through our Lord Jesus Christ. Therefore, my beloved brethren, be steadfast, immovable, always abounding in the work of the Lord, knowing that your toil is not in vain in the Lord.
>
> 1 Corinthians 15:53–58 (NASB)

Here at the end of Paul's refresher course on the resurrection, he identifies those who are included in the phrase "we shall all be changed" in verse 51. Those who will be changed "in the twinkling of an eye, at the last trumpet" include all church-age believers who are "steadfast, immovable, always abounding in the work of the Lord." The toil of these believers is not in vain but rather will result in their being changed instantly at the sound of the last trumpet. Every believer will ultimately also put on the imperishable and immortality. But those who have failed in being steadfast and immovable and abounding in work will not receive these things in such a glorious and once-in-eternity manner as being taken up at the gathering to Christ. Believers whose works after salvation are of the flesh and are in vain and useless will miss out. The reward of being taken before the start of the day of the Lord, and returning with Him at His second coming, is for believers who are motivated to obedience because they hold fast the word by which they are saved, and not rejecting the truth about the resurrection and the gathering. God has made the mystery of being gathered to Christ at the sound of the trumpet an integral part of the teaching of the resurrection.

> But now Christ has been raised from the dead, the first fruits of those who are asleep.
>
> 1 Corinthians 15:20 (NASB)

> But each in his own order: Christ the first fruits, after that those who are Christ's at His coming
>
> 1 Corinthians 15:23 (NASB)

As mentioned previously, being included in the gathering to Christ was also the motivation for labor and perseverance by the believers in the church at Thessalonica, 1 Thessalonians 1:6–10. With such a great hope, why did some of the Corinthian believers stop holding fast to the word and even started rejecting the teaching about the resurrection? They were attempting to rationalize their sinful lives. Paul commanded them to "stop sinning" in 1 Corinthians 15:34. These believers enjoyed living in sin and they wanted to eliminate the consequences for believers which are revealed in the teaching about the resurrection, such as being included or excluded at the gathering to Christ. If there is no resurrection, then there is no concern about any reward of being gathered to Christ. If there is no resurrection, then there is no accountability at any judgment seat, which Paul also mentions in this letter, 1 Corinthians 3:11–15. Those living in the flesh always feel more secure if they can get others to participate in the sin. Rebels are often deceived by the notion that there is strength in numbers, thinking that they can change a lie into the truth if they can get enough people to follow their evil. To motivate believers to follow his lead instead, Paul gives his own testimony with much humility to show that he also labors in a way so that his efforts are not in vain.

> And last of all, as it were to one untimely born, He appeared to me also.
>
> For I am the least of the apostles, who am not fit to be called an apostle, because I persecuted the church of God.
>
> But by the grace of God I am what I am, and His grace toward me did not prove vain; but I labored even more than all of them, yet not I, but the grace of God with me.
>
> Whether then it was I or they, so we preach and so you believed.
>
> 1 Corinthians 15:8–11 (NASB)

Paul is serving the Lord in a way that shows his determination that nothing in his life as an apostle of God will result in vanity. But he takes no credit for what he has accomplished, "yet not I."

Paul gives all the glory to God. By our own selves we are not able to produce anything of value, even after salvation, John 15:5.

"Hold fast the word" in 1 Corinthian 15:2 means to live in the reality of it. In 1 Corinthians 15:34, Paul commands those in Corinth who are living in sin to "become sober minded." Rejecting the truth, as some of the Corinth believers had done, does not change the reality of the truth. The gathering to Christ and the eternal rewards are very real and most wonderful. The rebuke and loss of eternal rewards are also very real and most regrettable. In the Revelation letter to the church in Philadelphia, John writes, "Because you have kept the word of My perseverance, I also will keep you from the hour of testing" (Revelation 3:10, NASB). Keeping the word of perseverance is the same thing as holding fast the word. Both Paul and John give these commands in the context of Jesus Christ coming to gather the faithful of the church. In the Philadelphia letter, John also makes use of the command "hold fast" with regard to receiving the reward of a crown.

> I am coming quickly; hold fast what you have, in order that no one take your crown.
>
> Revelation 3:11 (NASB)

Receiving a crown, reigning with Christ, being the bride of Christ, and being changed in a moment of time at the gathering to Christ are all associated. Believers will have either all or none of these blessings. In the next chapter, Scriptures will be examined that further clarify these principles.

Born again church-age believers who deny Jesus Christ a personal relationship in the temporal life will be left behind, whether they are physically alive or in the grave. They will still be members of the body of Christ, but they will not be included as part of the bride of Christ. The disobedient church-age believers who are alive will be left on the earth to suffer the horrors of Daniel's seventieth week. Some might think that those who are left in the graves will be the fortunate ones. However, those believers left alive on the earth will have one more opportunity to show themselves faithful in the midst of great suffering. They will still have the indwelling Holy Spirit. However, the restraining ability of the body of Christ left on the earth will be greatly diminished when the faithful of the church are removed at the gathering to Jesus Christ. Throughout the time of the church, it has been the faithful part of the body keeping in step with the Holy Spirit that has had the impact of being a restrainer. When Paul wrote about the church being the restrainer in 2 Thessalonians 2:7, he was writing to some of the most faithful believers of that time. Those of the church who continually walk in the flesh do not have the fruit of self control, Galatians 5:23. They are failing to be restrained themselves, so they certainly are not effective as any kind of hindrance to Satan. It will not be easy for the unfaithful church-age believers who are left behind to walk in obedience because degeneracy and apostasy of the world at that time will have an even stronger pull on their flesh natures. Also, Satan knows how he has been restrained throughout the time of the church by this residing presence of the Holy Spirit so his attacks against them will be relentless.

> It was granted to him to make war with the saints and to overcome them. And authority was given him over every tribe, tongue, and nation. All who dwell on the earth will worship him, whose names have not been written in the Book of Life of the Lamb slain from the foundation of the world. If anyone has an ear, let him hear. He who leads into captivity shall go into captivity; he who kills with the sword must be killed with the sword. Here is the patience and the faith of the saints.
>
> Revelation 13:7–10 (NKJV)

Those believers who finally become sober so that they walk in obedience are likely to be martyred, but as a result, they will receive the blessing of being resurrected at the end the tribulation to reign with Christ, to be included as the bride of Christ.

> Then I saw thrones, and they sat on them, and judgment was given to them. And I saw the souls of those who had been beheaded because of their testimony of Jesus and because of the word of God, and those who had not worshiped the beast or his image, and had not received the mark on their forehead and on their hand; and they came to life and reigned with Christ for a thousand years. The rest of the dead did not come to life until the thousand years were completed. This is the first resurrection. Blessed and holy is the one who has a part in the first resurrection; over these the second death has no power, but they will be priests of God and of Christ and will reign with Him for a thousand years.
>
> Revelation 20:4–6 (NASB)

DOMINION OF THE FAITHFUL

Since His return to the third heaven, Jesus has been in the process of preparing a place for His bride, John 14:2–3. Some biblical scholars have correctly made the point that there is no passage in the Bible that uses the words *bride* and *church* together. It is, however, a very reasonable conclusion that the church is being formed into the wife of Jesus Christ from what Paul wrote in 2 Corinthians 11:2–3, Ephesians 5:22–33, and Romans 7:1–6. These passages are not just symbolic.

The bride of Christ will be comprised of faithful believers who are asleep through Jesus along with the faithful believers who are still alive when the Lord returns to gather them off the earth. In Ephesians, Paul gives insight about how Christ has been in the process of forming His bride.

> Husbands, love your wives, just as Christ also loved the church and gave Himself up for her; that He might sanctify her, having cleansed her by the washing of water with the word, that He might present to Himself the church in all her glory, having no spot or wrinkle or any such thing; but that she should be holy and blameless.
>
> Ephesians 5:25–27 (NASB)

Christ wants to sanctify believers by the cleansing and washing with His Word. The transformation that takes place inside believers by God's Word is miraculous. To be very blunt, prior to salvation every human is impure and unholy like a prostitute before God. In this same letter to the Ephesus church, Paul reminds all believers from where they have come.

> And you were dead in your trespasses and sins, in which you formerly walked according to the course of this world, according to the prince of the power of the air, of the spirit that is now working in the sons of disobedience. Among them we too all formerly lived in the lusts of our flesh, indulging the desires of the flesh and of the mind, and were by nature children of wrath, even as the rest.
>
> Ephesians 2:1–3 (NASB)

Paul includes himself as one who was totally unacceptable to God. It is humanly impossible for a prostitute to be made into a chaste virgin, but that is exactly what God desires to accomplish inside every believer through the internal washing of His Word. To make sure that believers understand the crucial nature of this issue, Paul writes about the miraculous transformation accomplished through God's Word more than once in his Ephesians letter.

> And that you be renewed in the spirit of your mind, and put on the new self, which in the likeness of God has been created in righteousness and holiness of the truth.
>
> Ephesians 4:23–24 (NASB)

Being transformed into a chaste virgin for Jesus Christ happens simultaneously with being renewed in our minds so as to put on the new self, which is in the image of God. God has ordained that His powerful Word is the only means for this miracle to take place. Becoming the bride of Christ is a process that takes place only during the believer's temporal life after salvation. But the opportunity of being transformed into the bride of Christ also ends at physical death or at the gathering to Christ for the faithful who are still physically alive at His coming. Those who refuse to be cleansed by His Word do not receive the miraculous transformation inside. They continue to have spots and wrinkles and are not distinguishable from the filth that is in the world. Those believers will be excluded from being part of the chaste bride. Their neglect of being cleansed by the word will disqualify them.

The gathering to Christ before the apostasy is a reward for those who are faithful and worthy. Only those taken to meet the Lord in the air before the great wrath will have the awesome reward of being the bride of the Lamb and returning with Jesus Christ riding on white horses.

> Let us rejoice and be glad and give the glory to Him, for the marriage of the Lamb has come and His bride has made herself ready. And it was given to her to clothe herself in fine linen, bright and clean; for the fine linen is the righteous acts of the saints.
>
> Revelation 19:8 (NASB)

> And the armies which are in heaven, clothed in fine linen, white and clean, were following Him on white horses.
>
> Revelation 19:14 (NASB)

All the faithful believers from the whole church age are included as the bride of the Lamb. These are believers who have spent their temporal lives after salvation making themselves "ready" to be the bride. The process of making ourselves ready to be included as the bride has to take place now.

> For I am jealous for you with a godly jealousy; for I betrothed you to one husband, that to Christ I might present you as a pure virgin. But I am afraid, lest as the serpent deceived Eve by his craftiness, your minds should be led astray from the simplicity and purity of devotion to Christ.
>
> 2 Corinthians 11:2–3 (NASB)

We must be in the process of being miraculously transformed into a pure virgin for Christ in order for us to have the eternal honor of being the bride of the Lamb. The process of making ourselves ready does not begin when we get to heaven. That will be too late. It is crucial that we be in the process now of making ourselves "ready" by keeping our thoughts dwelling on the simplicity and purity of Christ, which is accomplished only by continuously feeding our minds on the Word of God. The putting on of the bright and clean, fine linen is only the end of the process. The very last thing a bride does in preparing herself for her wedding is put on her wedding dress. The bright and clean linen put on by the bride of the Lamb is "the righteous acts of the saints." All those of the church who are gathered out of the graves and those taken alive by Jesus Christ are those who have carried out righteous acts in their temporal lives after salvation. There will be no use for believers who walk in unrighteousness to be taken by the Lord at this time because there will be no clothing for them. Satan cannot undo any believer's eternal salvation. But Satan desires to and can seduce believers away from devotion to Christ to prevent them from achieving the honor of being the pure virgin bride of the Lamb. All believers need to take a personal account and ask themselves if they are willing to let the devil rob them of this eternal position of unfathomable blessing. Imagine being the bride and wife of the Creator and Sustainer of the entire universe. The bright and clean fine linen given to the faithful of the church is only the beginning of the rewards and benefits they will receive.

In his second letter to Timothy, Paul reveals that the unfaithful believers of the church will be denied the reward of reigning with Christ.

> It is a trustworthy statement: For if we died with Him, we shall also live with Him; If we endure, we shall also reign with Him; If we deny Him, He also will deny us; If we are faithless, He remains faithful; for He cannot deny Himself.
>
> 2 Timothy 2:11–13 (NASB)

Believers who endure are those who are faithful to Jesus Christ and they will reign with Him. Those who "deny Him" are believers who are faithless to Jesus Christ and as a result "He also will deny" them the reward of reigning with Him. Jesus Christ does not deny faithless believers eternal life because "He cannot deny Himself." Every believer of the church is eternally a part of the body of Christ. He will amputate no members.

Believers who are given the reward of reigning with Christ are also those who will be the bride of Christ. They are associated. According to Paul, the relationship between Jesus and the church is a great mystery that is analogous to the relationship between Adam and Eve.

> He who loves his own wife loves himself; for no one ever hated his own flesh, but nourishes and cherishes it, just as Christ also does the church, because we are members of His body. For this cause a man shall leave his father and mother, and shall cleave to his wife; and the two shall become one flesh. This mystery is great; but I am speaking with reference to Christ and the church.
>
> Ephesians 5:28–32 (NASB)

The statement about a man leaving his father and mother and cleaving to his wife to be come one flesh with her was first used of Adam and Eve. Jesus Christ is the "last Adam," 1 Corinthians 15:45. The bride of Christ is destined to reign and share dominion on the earth with the last Adam just as Eve shared dominion with the first Adam, Genesis 1:27–28 and 2 Timothy 2:12. Here is the mega-mystery. The entire church is the body of Christ. As Eve was formed out of the being of Adam, so the bride of Christ will be formed out of the being of the Christ. The gathering of certain members of the body of Christ from the earth is the equivalent to the removal of the rib from the body of Adam. As Eve was formed from the rib removed from Adam, so the bride of Christ will be formed out of the portion of the body of Christ removed off the earth at the gathering. Not all the body will be taken, but only a portion as only the rib of Adam was used to form Eve. Only the faithful of the body of Christ will comprise the rib of His body that will be used to form the bride. The piercing of Jesus Christ in the side by the spear near to His rib at the crucifixion symbolizes that His death opened the way for the bride of Christ to be formed. The bride of Christ will be taken out of the body of Christ and will be reattached to Christ in a personal and intimate and eternal relationship.

> Then we who are alive and remain shall be caught up together with them in the clouds to meet the Lord in the air, and thus we shall always be with the Lord.
>
> 1 Thessalonians 4:17 (NASB)

When the faithful believers are gathered out of the body, "thus they shall always be with the Lord." All who are of the body of Christ will forever be His body. But only the faithful portion of the body will be given the amazing reward of being the bride and eternal wife of Jesus Christ.

The loss of rewards will be regrettable to unfaithful believers, but the most sorrowful aspect of their judgment will come from personally looking face-to-face at the loving Savior who was so deserving of their loyalty.

> And now, little children, abide in Him, so that when He appears, we may have confidence and not shrink away from Him in shame at His coming. If you know that He is righteous, you know that everyone also who practices righteousness is born of Him. See how great a love the Father has bestowed upon us, that we should be called children of God; and such we are. For this reason the world does not know us, because it did not know Him. Beloved, now we are children of God, and it has not appeared as yet what we shall be. We know that, when He appears, we shall be like Him, because we shall see Him just as He is. And everyone who has this hope fixed on Him purifies himself, just as He is pure.
>
> 1 John 2:28–3:3 (NASB)

As in Paul's letters, so also John calls the appearing of Jesus Christ our "hope." Believers are purified when they live in anticipation of the Lord's physical appearance. They are purified because they live so as to be continuously ready at any moment to see the Lord. Christians who fail to hold to this hope are not purified, having no regard to whether they are living in a manner worthy of Jesus Christ. There are three different appearances of Jesus Christ given in the prophecies in which humans are resurrected and come face-to-face with their Creator. His first appearing for resurrection is to gather the faithful, per 1 Thessalonians 4 and 1 Corinthians 15. His second appearing for resurrection is at His second coming, per Revelation 20:4–6. His third appearing for resurrection is when He is seated on the great white throne, per Revelation 20:11–15. All the believers who see Jesus "just as He is" at His first appearing are those who have the confidence that John writes about. Believers who live in righteousness can be confident they will be included in this event when Jesus Christ comes to take His eternal bride. The resurrection of unfaithful believers is covered in the last chapter, "The Eternal City of God." The appearance of Jesus Christ emanates holiness. Believers who have not endeavored to become holy and blameless after salvation will not "be like him" when He appears, and they will be ashamed when they see the holiness of the Lord. Believers who fail to fix their hope on seeing Jesus "just as He is" have no sense of an urgent need to be purified in their temporal lives. The phrase "we shall be like Him" is not referring to having an external resurrection body like Jesus. It is well documented in Scripture that God is not concerned about and does not look upon the external. The addition of the resurrection body is just the finishing touch on the transformation that is to be taking place throughout our lives after salvation. The children who will have confidence "at His coming" are the believers who have been diligent in the transformation to be like Jesus Christ on the inside: Ephesians 4:20–24, Romans 8:29 and 13:14, Colossians 3:10, Galatians 2:20, and 2 Corinthians 4:10. These believers will be "confident" because they have known the Lord personally and intimately from their faithful walk with Him since becoming engaged to Him at salvation. The appearing of the Lord, seeing Him as He is in all His holy radiance, and being made to be like Him in eternal resurrection bodies will be a most blessed and incredible event for faithful believers. When Jesus Christ calls them to Himself and they meet Him in the air, they will see Him as their bridegroom coming to take them to be His eternal bride. Each believer's temporal life after salvation is their own personal betrothal period to the Lord. A groom will not follow through with the marriage if the betrothed has been unfaithful. Jesus Christ rightly desires and He most deserves to have only a holy and blameless pure virgin to be His bride. In the Jewish culture, a man and woman were legally bound together at the time of the engagement. A divorce was required to legally break the engagement. This is evident in the account of Joseph wanting to put away Mary after he discovered she was with child before they had consummated their marriage, Matthew 1:18–19. According to Jesus, adultery is the only acceptable cause for divorce, Matthew 5:32 and 19:9. God described His punishment of Israel as His divorcing them for their idolatry, which is adultery to God, Jeremiah 3:8. God hates divorce, Malachi 2:16. Jesus does not want to divorce any believer. God always desires reconciliation first and foremost, but Jesus will not remain betrothed to believers who fail to repent and turn from the continuous practice of adultery. Church-age believers who continually walk in the flesh after salvation are as guilty of adultery as was Israel. These are the ones who will be "ashamed before Him at His coming." They too will see Jesus Christ "just as He is" when they are resurrected and stand before His judgment seat. Because they were unfaithful in their betrothal period, they will be excluded when the Lord comes to gather His bride. These believers will also be made to be like Jesus Christ, having resurrection bodies, but that will be their only eternal asset. They will suffer the loss of eternal rewards and be saved as though by fire, 1 Corinthians 3:15. They are still saved, but they will be ashamed as is an unfaithful woman when her betrothed discovers her unfaithfulness, and the wedding is permanently cancelled. The shame will be such that they will want to find a place to hide, but there will be no place to hide as every believer will have to stand openly before the judgment seat of Jesus Christ. The appearing of Jesus Christ and the reality of seeing Him face-to-face just as He is in His radiant glory and holiness will not be pleasant for believers who lived their temporal lives in a manner unworthy of His sacrifice on the cross for them. Those believers will experience fear in the Lord's judgment.

By this, love is perfected with us, that we may have confidence in the day of judgment; because as He is, so also are we in this world. There is no fear in love; but perfect love casts out fear, because fear involves punishment, and the one who fears is not perfected in love.

1 John 4:17–18 (NASB)

The manifestation of self-sacrificing love in a believer's life is a sure sign they are walking in fellowship with Jesus Christ by the power of the Holy Spirit. Here again the Apostle John writes about having confidence in the day of the Lord's judgment. Believers who walk in obedience by the power of the Holy Spirit will be perfected in love. Love is the first of the fruit of the Spirit, Galatians 5:22. Those who are perfected in love will have absolutely no fear of the day of judgment. The love casts out fear as it is related to the coming judgment, so they will have only confidence. Those who do not have love perfected in them will have fear of punishment, which is the loss of eternal rewards. Because they will have spent a majority of their time after salvation continuing to walk in the flesh, the Spirit will have had no opportunity to perfect love in them. The Holy Spirit desires to do His miraculous work inside every believer to keep us from having to experience the ominous fear at the judgment seat of Jesus Christ. In order for the Spirit of God to accomplish the inner transformation, we must each be willing to be led by the Spirit.

For all who are being led by the Spirit of God, these are sons of God. For you have not received a spirit of slavery leading to fear again, but you have received a spirit of adoption as sons by which we cry out, "Abba! Father!"

Romans 8:14–15 (NASB)

Believers who fail to give themselves over to the Holy Spirit are depriving themselves the wonder of living as sons of God and having the assurance that comes from a personal relationship with the heavenly Father.

As noted previously, Paul calls the relationship of Jesus Christ with His bride a great mystery.

> For this cause a man shall leave his father and mother, and shall cleave to his wife; and the two shall become one flesh. This mystery is great; but I am speaking with reference to Christ and the church.
>
> Ephesians 5:31–32 (NASB)

Paul uses the word *mystery* fifteen times when referring to the church age in his epistles. In 1 Corinthians 15:51, Paul calls the resurrection and gathering of the faithful to Christ a mystery. The correlation of the relationship of Christ and the church as that of a husband and wife is the only aspect of the church mystery that Paul refers to as being mega or great. Most often Paul refers to the mystery in reference to the fact that the church age was hidden in times past.

> By revelation there was made known to me the mystery, as I wrote before in brief. By referring to this, when you read you can understand my insight into the mystery of Christ, which in other generations was not made known to the sons of men, as it has now been revealed to His holy apostles and prophets in the Spirit.
>
> Ephesians 3:3–5 (NASB)

> To me, the very least of all saints, this grace was given, to preach to the Gentiles the unfathomable riches of Christ, and to bring to light what is the administration of the mystery which for ages has been hidden in God who created all things.
>
> Ephesians 3:8–9 (NASB)

In Ephesians 3:5, Paul writes that the mystery was not made known, which can also be translated the mystery was not recognized by past generations. Paul is not communicating that information about the mystery was not given, but that the information was hidden so not to be recognized. There is information about the great mystery that was recorded by the Old Testament prophets. Just as the prophecies about the suffering of Messiah were hidden but have now come to light, so also the prophecies about the great mystery were hidden. One of Paul's duties was to bring to light the hidden information. It is assumed by many believers that the great mystery of the Christ and His bride is fully understood. There are, however, a variety of interpretations about the bride of Christ and about the prophecies concerning His gathering of the faithful, so the mystery is not really fully understood. There are some Christians who believe Israel is the bride of Christ based on numerous Old Testament passages like Isaiah 54:5, Jeremiah 2:2, and the gospel passages Matthew 9:15 and John 3:29. Bringing to light the great mystery of the bride and the mystery of the gathering to Christ requires more extensive study and the comparing of Scripture with Scripture, including the Old Testament prophets.

When the Apostle Paul writes about the gathering of the faithful in the letters to the Thessalonica and Corinthian churches, he was countering false teachings about the resurrection and the timing of Christ's coming. Paul was giving refresher courses on these subjects that he had communicated to the churches verbally in more detail and depth when he was present with them, 1 Corinthian 15:3, 12 and 2 Thessalonians 2:5. Interestingly, there is a story in the Old Testament that further reinforces the mystery teachings of the church age that the gathering of believers by Jesus Christ is conditional on their faithfulness and obedience.

Then Enoch walked with God three hundred years...

And Enoch walked with God; and he was not, for God took him.

Genesis 5:22 and 24 (NASB)

By faith Enoch was taken up so that he should not see death; and he was not found because God took him up; for he obtained the witness that before his being taken up he was pleasing to God.

Hebrews 11:5 (NASB)

The account of Enoch sets a precedent in Scripture about who God considers worthy to be taken off the earth without seeing death. The taking up of Enoch was a reward for his having obtained a witness on the earth that he was pleasing to God. So also, the taking of church age believers off the earth without seeing death will be a reward to obedient believers who are alive at the time Jesus returns to gather the faithful. As covered in the previous chapter, there is much evidence in the New Testament prophecies that the gathering to Christ is conditional. Those faithful believers will be included with those who will be the bride of Christ. It is prudent for every believer to be all the more vigilant to ensure that we are walking with the Lord.

There is another Old Testament prophecy written by the sons of Korah that gives light to the great mystery. In Hebrews 1:8–9, the New Testament writer quotes part of this prophecy given in Psalm 45 when writing about the coming kingdom of Jesus Christ. In this prophecy is a mysterious reference to a queen.

³Gird Your sword on Your thigh, O Mighty One, In Your splendor and Your majesty!

⁴And in Your majesty ride on victoriously, for the cause of truth and meekness and righteousness; Let Your right hand teach You awesome things.

⁵Your arrows are sharp; The peoples fall under You; *Your arrows are* in the heart of the King's enemies.

⁶Your throne, O God, is forever and ever; A scepter of uprightness is the scepter of Your kingdom.

⁷You have loved righteousness and hated wickedness; Therefore God, Your God, has anointed You With the oil of joy above Your fellows.

⁸All Your garments are fragrant with myrrh and aloes and cassia; Out of ivory palaces stringed instruments have made You glad.

⁹Kings' daughters are among your noble ladies; At Your right hand stands the queen in gold from Ophir.

¹⁰Listen, O daughter, give attention and incline your ear: Forget your people and your father's house;

¹¹Then the King will desire your beauty. Because He is your Lord, bow down to Him.

¹²The daughter of Tyre will come with a gift; The rich among the people will seek your favor.

¹³The King's daughter is all glorious within; Her clothing is interwoven with gold.

¹⁴She will be led to the King in embroidered work; The virgins, her companions who follow her, will be brought to You.

¹⁵They will be led forth with gladness and rejoicing; They will enter into the King's palace.

Psalm 45:3–15 (NASB)

Verses 3 through 5 are prophecy about the second coming of Jesus Christ riding in splendor and majesty against His enemies on the earth. After the Lord defeats His enemies, then He will reign on the earth as prophesied in Verses 6 and 8. Verse 8 foretells that the garments of Jesus Christ will have the fragrance of myrrh and aloes and cassia, which are fragrances used for burial. These are the ingredients that Nicodemus brought to anoint the body of the eternal King after His death on the cross. As the peoples of the nations go to worship the Lord and seek His counsel during the kingdom age, this fragrance will be a continual reminder of the Lord's sacrificial death. In verse 9 the prophecy jumps ahead to the eternal estate in the New Jerusalem. At the right hand of the Lord Jesus Christ will stand a queen who is adorned in gold. The identity of this queen is a mystery. Some would say it is Israel, and others would say it is the church. Proceeding with the premise that the queen is the bride of Christ, then the identity of the bride of Christ is also a mystery. In verses 10 and 11, an exhortation is given to her to leave behind her father's house. This is a call to believers to relinquish the desires of the flesh by abandoning the lustful pursuits of the things this world. If she does, then the King will desire her beauty. The King in verse 11 is Jesus Christ. In verse 10 and 13, the queen is referred to as "daughter." The queen, the bride of Christ, is also the daughter of God the Father. In verse 13 the queen is called "the King's daughter." God the Father and God the Son are both the eternal King.

> Then the seventh angel sounded; and there were loud voices in heaven, saying, "The kingdom of the world has become the kingdom of our Lord and of His Christ; and He will reign forever and ever."
>
> Revelation 11:15 (NASB)

> Then he showed me a river of the water of life, clear as crystal, coming from the throne of God and of the Lamb.
>
> Revelation 22:1 (NASB)

Both God the Father and God the Son will occupy the throne in the New Jerusalem. In Psalm 45, the title "King" is used of both God the Father and God the Son. In verse 11, King is referring to God the Son. In verse 13, "King" is referring to God the Father. In verse 14, "King" is referring to God the Son. This is determined by the last phrase in the verse: "Will be brought to You." All the pronouns *You* and *Your* in Psalm 45 are God the Father speaking to God the Son.

Some of the other psalms along with the prophets Isaiah, Jeremiah, Micah, Zephaniah, and Zechariah refer to the people of Israel as the "daughter of Zion" and the "daughter of Jerusalem."

> As for you, tower of the flock, Hill of the daughter of Zion,
> to you it will come, even the former dominion will come,
> the kingdom of the daughter of Jerusalem.
>
> Micah 4:8 (NASB)

The "former dominion" refers to the absolute dominion of God as it was at the beginning of the creation. The former dominion will be reestablished with the coming of the new heaven and the new earth and the New Jerusalem. The "Zion" and the "Jerusalem" referred to in this prophesy are the eternal New Mt. Zion and the eternal New Jerusalem on the new earth. The "daughter of Zion" and the "daughter of Jerusalem" are both designations for the bride of Christ, the queen in gold from Ophir. The kingdom is called "the kingdom of the daughter of Jerusalem" because it is given to her to eternally share in the dominion as a reward for her faithfulness to her Beloved. It was not uncommon for human kings to offer up to half their kingdom to women who greatly pleased them, Esther 5:3 and Mark 6:23. Psalm 45 is another passage giving evidence that the queen bride is Israel, since it was prophecy written to Israel. It is evident that Israel and Judah are betrothed to the Lord. But it is also evident in the New Testament writings of Paul that the church is the bride of Christ. That brings up the question whether the Lord Jesus has two wives. God has never condoned polygamy. In 1 Corinthians 7:2–4, the wording used by Paul makes it clear that God intends each man to have only one wife and each woman to have only one husband. The great mystery is that the bride of Christ will include faithful believers from the age of Israel and from the age of the church. The Lord has only one bride. Additionally, the great mystery is that the Lord has been in the process of forming His eternal bride from faithful believers throughout human history. In order to establish a starting point on the topic of the prophecy about Jesus returning to gather His bride, it was necessary to address it from the perspective of the faithful church only. Now it can be revealed that this event includes all faithful believers of human history up through the end of the church age. When Christ returns to gather the faithful from the earth, He will resurrect all those who have been faithful believers going back to Adam and Eve, to make them His eternal bride. Enoch was the first to be taken in this manner as an example to all believers in every age as to the expectation. Paul's descriptions of Christ appearing to gather His bride in 1 Thessalonians 4, and 2 Thessalonians 2, and 1 Corinthians 15 do not exclude believers who lived prior to the church age. In His plan for human history, God has established dispensations or phases. In each dispensation God gives a new level of revelation about His plan that centers around His Son, Jesus Christ. A common theme in all dispensations is that salvation from the lake of fire is a gift given on the basis of faith alone, and that works are the means to eternal rewards. For example, Abraham's salvation was through faith and not works, Romans 4:1–25. However, Abraham's honor of being called a friend of God and being justified to receive eternal rewards is based on his works after salvation, James 2:21–24. The highest honor and reward is being the bride of Christ. There are other evidences of these truths in the writings of the Old Testament prophets.

Just as Paul writes about the relationship between the Lord and the church being analogous to a husband-wife relationship, so also Isaiah, Jeremiah, Ezekiel, and Hosea all write about the relationship between the Lord and Israel and Judah being analogous to a husband-wife relationship. This is no coincidence, but is the deliberate intent of the Holy Spirit who inspired the writers of these Old and New Testament Scriptures.

> Now the word of the Lord came to me saying, "Go and proclaim in the ears of Jerusalem, saying, 'Thus says the Lord, "I remember concerning you the devotion of your youth, the love of your betrothals, your following after Me in the wilderness, through a land not sown.
>
> Jeremiah 2:1–2 (NASB)

> Can a virgin forget her ornaments, or a bride her attire? Yet My people have forgotten Me Days without number.
>
> Jeremiah 2:32 (NASB)

> And I saw that for all the adulteries of faithless Israel, I had sent her away and given her a writ of divorce, yet her treacherous sister Judah did not fear; but she went and was a harlot also.
>
> Jeremiah 3:8 (NASB)

> "Surely, as a woman treacherously departs from her lover, so you have dealt treacherously with Me, O house of Israel," declares the Lord.
>
> Jeremiah 3:20 (NASB)

> What right has My beloved in My house when she has done many vile deeds? Can the sacrificial flesh take away from you your disaster, so *that* you can rejoice?
>
> Jeremiah 11:15 (NASB)

All of these passages refer to the relationship that Judah and Israel had with the Lord, meaning the preincarnate Jesus Christ.

It was the preincarnate Lord who was in the glory cloud with Israel in the wilderness. During that time, Israel was betrothed to the Lord, Jeremiah 2:2. But the generation of Israel (the northern kingdom) during the time of Isaiah became very degenerate because of idolatry, so God gave that generation a divorce, Jeremiah 3:8. The same thing happened to Judah (the southern kingdom) during the time of Jeremiah and Ezekiel.

> When you built your shrine at the beginning of every street and made your high place in every square, in disdaining money, you were not like a harlot. You adulteress wife, who takes strangers instead of her husband!
>
> Ezekiel 16:31–32 (NASB)

> You are the daughter of your mother, who loathed her husband and children. You are also the sister of your sisters, who loathed their husbands and children. Your mother was a Hittite and your father an Amorite.
>
> Ezekiel 16:45 (NASB)

It is important to understand that the Lord did not divorce all of Israel going back to Abraham, Isaac, and Jacob. A majority of the people of Israel and Judah from the time of Isaiah to the time of Jeremiah were idolatrous, so the Lord divorced those generations of Jews. However, some of God's most faithful servants from the age of Israel were also in that generation, including Isaiah, Hezekiah, Josiah, Jeremiah, Ezekiel, Daniel, and many others. Although the Lord divorced the adulteress-idolatrous believers in those generations of Judah and Israel, the faithful of Judah and Israel will still have the eternal blessing of being the wife of the Lord.

> Thus says the LORD, "Where is the certificate of divorce by which I have sent your mother away? Or to whom of My creditors did I sell you? Behold, you were sold for your

iniquities, and for your transgressions your mother was sent away."

Isaiah 50:1 (NASB)

"Fear not, for you will not be put to shame; and do not feel humiliated, for you will not be disgraced; But you will forget the shame of your youth, and the reproach of your widowhood you will remember no more. "For your husband is your Maker, Whose name is the Lord of hosts; and your Redeemer is the Holy One of Israel, Who is called the God of all the earth. "For the Lord has called you, like a wife forsaken and grieved in spirit, even like a wife of one's youth when she is rejected," Says your God.

Isaiah 54:4–6 (NASB)

Faithful Israel will be included in the eternal reward blessing of being the bride of Christ. Paul makes it very clear that God has not abandoned nor rejected faithful Israel. But for unfaithful Israel, there are consequences, as there are for unfaithful believers in every age of human history.

What then? What Israel is seeking, it has not obtained, but those who were chosen obtained it, and the rest were hardened.

Romans 11:7 (NASB)

The forming of the bride of Christ will continue through the thousand-year kingdom of Christ, so the bride will not be complete till the end of that period. The forming of the bride will be partially complete when Jesus Christ gathers the faithful saints from the earth before the time of the seven-year tribulation period, but more faithful believers will be added from the tribulation period and from the thousand-year kingdom age.

Another prophetic topic that corroborates with to this statement is the prophecies about an eternal priesthood.

The first time that God spoke about creating a ruling kingdom of priests on earth was at Mt Sinai when He expressed to Moses this desire for the nation Israel.

> "'Now then, if you will indeed obey My voice and keep My covenant, then you shall be My own possession among all the peoples, for all the earth is Mine; and you shall be to Me a kingdom of priests and a holy nation.' These are the words that you shall speak to the sons of Israel."
>
> Exodus 19:5–6 (NASB)

God has not yet fulfilled this expressed desire of Israel. That is because, like the forming of the bride, this too has been a work of God in progress. Peter brings this prophecy forward into the church age and applies it to the church.

> But you are a chosen race, a royal priesthood, a holy nation, a people for God's own possession, so that you may proclaim the excellencies of Him who has called you out of darkness into His marvelous light; for you once were not a people, but now you are the people of God; you had not received mercy, but now you have received mercy.
>
> 1 Peter 2:9–10 (NASB)

Some have said that Peter is writing this to the early church only, which consisted of Jews, since God originally communicated this declaration to Moses for Israel. Others have said that since Israel failed the Jews have forfeited this blessing and it now belongs to the church. A prophecy in Revelation gives further illumination.

> And they sang a new song, saying, "Worthy are You to take the book and to break its seals; for You were slain, and

purchased for God with Your blood men from every tribe and tongue and people and nation. "You have made them to be a kingdom and priests to our God; and they will reign upon the earth."

Revelation 5:9–10 (NASB)

It is obvious that God has always intended that the kingdom of priests will include believers from every race and nationality. Just as the bride of Christ is being formed with faithful believers from throughout human history, so also the kingdom of priests is being formed with faithful believers from all of human history. The bride of Christ is the kingdom of royal priests, the chosen race, the holy nation. Martyrs from the tribulation period will be resurrected and add to this elite group at the start of the thousand-year kingdom of Christ.

Then I saw thrones, and they sat on them, and judgment was given to them. And I *saw* the souls of those who had been beheaded because of their testimony of Jesus and because of the word of God, and those who had not worshiped the beast or his image, and had not received the mark on their forehead and on their hand; and they came to life and reigned with Christ for a thousand years. The rest of the dead did not come to life until the thousand years were completed. This is the first resurrection. Blessed and holy is the one who has a part in the first resurrection; over these the second death has no power, but they will be priests of God and of Christ and will reign with Him for a thousand years.

Revelation 20:4–6 (NASB)

This is prophecy about the faithful believers from the tribulation period who will be resurrected and added to the bride of Christ to reign with Christ when He returns to vanquish His enemies and establish His thousand-year kingdom.

Information that Jesus communicated to the Sadducees gives further confirmation that being included in the gathering to Christ and having a place in His coming kingdom are conditional. The Sadducees taught heresy by proclaiming that there is no resurrection from the dead. They had a plot to trap Jesus on this issue in order to discredit Him. The answer that Jesus gave them is very telling of who will be included and who will be excluded from the resurrection and His thousand-year kingdom.

> [34]Jesus said to them, "The sons of this age marry and are given in marriage, [35]but those who are considered worthy to attain to that age and the resurrection from the dead, neither marry nor are given in marriage; [36]for they cannot even die anymore, because they are like angels, and are sons of God, being sons of the resurrection.
>
> Luke 20:34-36 (NASB)

Jesus begins His response to the Sadducees by affirming marriage is practiced while still in this temporal life. In verse 35 Jesus reveals that marriage will not be practiced in the resurrection. Additionally, the response from Jesus reveals that being included in the resurrection leading to "that age" has to be attained. "That age" is referring to His coming thousand-year kingdom. The Greek word Jesus uses, translated *attain*, is different than the Greek work Paul uses in Philippians 3:11, also translated *attain*. The word Jesus uses is a stronger word that emphasizes hitting the mark or to become master of something. This accentuates Jesus's statement that it is necessary to be considered worthy. Those who attain a place in the kingdom will be included in the resurrection. Those who do not attain a place in the kingdom will not be included in the resurrection. In verse 36 the ones who are included in the resurrection are called "sons of the resurrection." This is a unique and special title for those who are considered worthy. Obviously this resurrection has to occur before the start of the kingdom age. The resurrection Jesus refers to when responding to the Sadducees is the same gathering of His faithful before the start of the end-time tribulation that Paul describes in his letters to the churches at Thessalonica and Corinth. Jesus communicated this truth to Jews who were living in the age of Israel. The resurrection when Jesus returns to gather the faithful will include the faithful of the church, but it is not for the church only. Additionally, reigning with Christ in the Kingdom Age is also not for the church only. Prophecy about the saints reigning with Christ was first given to Israel in the Old Testament.

> Then the sovereignty, the dominion and the greatness of *all* the kingdoms under the whole heaven will be given to the people of the saints of the Highest One; His kingdom *will be* an everlasting kingdom, and all the dominions will serve and obey Him.
>
> Daniel 7:27 (NASB)

Faithful believers from the age of Israel will reign with Jesus Christ in the coming Kingdom Age, as will faithful believers from the church age and every dispensation of human history.

Certainly it is much more desirable to be included with those who are the first of the human race to be resurrected from the dead and to enter the coming kingdom as the bride of Christ with an abundance of rewards provided to us, as Peter writes.

> [5]Now for this very reason also, applying all diligence, in your faith supply moral excellence, and in *your* moral excellence, knowledge, [6]and in *your* knowledge, self-control, and in *your* self-control, perseverance, and in *your* perseverance, godliness, [7]and in *your* godliness, brotherly kindness, and in *your* brotherly kindness, love.
>
> [8]For if these *qualities* are yours and are increasing, they render you neither useless nor unfruitful in the true knowledge of our Lord Jesus Christ.

⁹For he who lacks these *qualities* is blind *or* short-sighted, having forgotten *his* purification from his former sins.

¹⁰Therefore, brethren, be all the more diligent to make certain about His calling and choosing you; for as long as you practice these things, you will never stumble; ¹¹for in this way the entrance into the eternal kingdom of our Lord and Savior Jesus Christ will be abundantly supplied to you.

2 Peter 1:5–11 (NASB)

In verses 5–7 Peter describes a character that closely parallels the character that is described by Paul as the fruit of the Spirit in Galatians 5:22–23. Members of the body of Christ need not wait until the New Jerusalem to eat the fruit of the tree of life, which is the fruit of the Spirit. Putting to death the works of one's flesh nature and living life characterized by the fruit of the Spirit is a very powerful and unique blessing given to every believer now, while still living in this temporal life. Unbelievers have no inherent resources to gain such freedom because the flesh cannot put itself to death. The flesh is a ball and chain that every human drags around. Only the believer has the potential of being free from this encumbrance. Every believer in Jesus Christ has been given the holy and omnipotent resource necessary. In 2 Peter 1:8, Peter writes that these qualities need to be increasing. Believers are never to be content with their level of maturity, but must keep seeking after and growing closer to the Lord. Peter also writes that doing this will keep the believer from becoming useless and unfruitful. In order to be continuously fruitful, the believer must be growing in the true knowledge of Jesus Christ. The fruit of the Spirit is the character of Jesus Christ. Growing in this character is the same as increasing in the true knowledge of Him. According to Peter, the believer who fails in growing in their relationship with Jesus Christ is "short-sighted," verse 9.

They are short-sighted to the eternal and the abundant rewards they could obtain, verse 11.

> So then, brethren, we are under obligation, not to the flesh, to live according to the flesh— for if you are living according to the flesh, you must die; but if by the Spirit you are putting to death the deeds of the body, you will live.
>
> Romans 8:12–13 (NASB)

> But I say, walk by the Spirit, and you will not carry out the desire of the flesh. For the flesh sets its desire against the Spirit, and the Spirit against the flesh; for these are in opposition to one another, so that you may not do the things that you please.
>
> Galatians 5:16–17 (NASB)

To be included as part of the bride of Christ and to share in the absolute dominion of Christ, the believer must be living in the power of the Holy Spirit so as to put to death the deeds of the flesh. The fearful warnings to the children of God about the loss of rewards and being excluded at the gathering to Jesus Christ are foreboding only to those who continually have no care whether they are walking in the light or the darkness. Paul makes it clear in other letters that all believers, including himself, must be faithful until death to obtain the rewards and to assure their place in this resurrection, 2 Timothy 4:6–8 and 1 Corinthians 9:26–27. God has provided a checklist whereby every member of the body of Christ can determine whether they will be included or excluded from being the bride.

> Now the deeds of the flesh are evident, which are: immorality, impurity, sensuality, idolatry, sorcery, enmities, strife, jealousy, outbursts of anger, disputes, dissensions, factions, envying, drunkenness, carousing, and things like these, of which I forewarn you just as I have forewarned

you that those who practice such things shall not inherit the kingdom of God.

Galatians 5:19–21 (NASB)

"Inherit the kingdom of God" is not the same as receiving salvation from the eternal lake of fire, which is given as a gift at the point of faith in Jesus Christ. The inheritance refers to eternal rewards such as being included with the faithful church that the Lord will gather off the earth and out of the wrath to come and receiving the honor of being the bride of Christ.

The promises at the end of each of the seven letters from Jesus Christ to each of the churches in Revelation 2 and 3 are rewards for those who are the bride of Christ, the royal priests, the holy nation. Only the faithful of the church who overcome will have a vital role with Jesus Christ in sharing His dominion on the earth.

> He who overcomes, I will grant to him to sit down with Me on My throne, as I also overcame and sat down with My Father on His throne.
>
> Revelation 3:21 (NASB)

The faithful believers are promised to be given authority over the nations to rule them with a rod of iron along with the Lord Jesus Christ.

> Nevertheless what you have, hold fast until I come. And he who overcomes, and he who keeps My deeds until the end, to him I will give authority over the nations; and he shall rule them with a rod of iron, as the vessels of the potter are broken to pieces, as I also have received authority from My Father; and I will give him the morning star.
>
> Revelation 2:25–28 (NASB)

This promise to believers who "overcome" is one of the reasons that Satan hates faithful believers so much. Satan's original name was Lucifer, meaning "star of the morning" or "morning star," Isaiah 14:12. The Son of God also has that title.

> I, Jesus, have sent My angel to testify to you these things for the churches. I am the root and the offspring of David, the bright morning star.
>
> Revelation 22:16 (NASB)

The title "morning star" designates some aspect of authority and power. Lucifer was given the blessing of sharing that title with the Son of God, who has always been the "bright morning star." When Lucifer rebelled, he was stripped of that title and the power. At His judgment seat, Jesus Christ will reward the faithful believers who have overcome with the privileges and rights of the morning star. This honor that once belonged to the most powerful angelic being is going to be given to humans. Additionally, those who overcome will also be given authority on the earth to reign with Jesus Christ. The faithful believers of the church and those from all of human history are going to share in the absolute dominion that Satan wants so desperately for himself.

> Will you still say before him who slays you, "I am god"? But you shall be a man, and not a god, in the hand of him who slays you.
>
> Ezekiel 28:9 (NKJV)

DOING ALL TO STAND FIRM

The death of Jesus Christ on the cross and His resurrection from the dead was the decisive victory in the war for dominion in heaven and on the earth. As mentioned previously, after the resurrection Jesus told His disciples that all authority had been given to Him in heaven and on the earth, Matthew 28:18. Surely Satan did not know what to expect next. He knew that Israel had rejected Jesus as the Messiah, and that the rejection continued even after the resurrection and the ascension, Acts 28:24–31. Israel's continued rejection must have been a glimmer of hope to Satan. It appeared that God no longer had a nation and a people on the earth that represented Him, and Satan continued to have control of the nations. God had promised Israel that He would make a new covenant with them, Jeremiah 31:31–34, but He could not enter into a new covenant with those who rejected His Messiah. God had a mystery in His plan, however, to create a new and unique body of people on the earth called the church, Ephesians 3:4–10. Like Jesus, this mystery group of people would be empowered by the omnipotent Holy Spirit, by whom the body is able to manifest even greater miracles than those done by Jesus, John 14:12. The Word of God and the Holy Spirit function as the central nervous system of the body that enable the members of the body worldwide to be connected to and sensitive to directives of the Head, Jesus Christ, Ephesians 4:11–16.

Jesus was making preparations for the establishment of this new entity during His three years of ministry. Even before the crucifixion and before the disciples had received the Holy Spirit, they were given power over Satan's forces.

> And He called the twelve together, and gave them power and authority over all the demons, and to heal diseases.
>
> Luke 9:1 (NASB)

Think of the horror this must have caused Satan and the fallen angelic realm when they saw beings made from the dust of the ground exercising such decisive and absolute power and authority over the forces of darkness. This had never happened before in all the history of creation. The satanic powers had always had the advantage in their dealings with humans. It was expected that the Son of God would have power over demons, but it was not anticipated that humans would have such power. Then Jesus sent out a larger number of disciples with power over Satan's demonic forces by simply commanding them in His name.

> The seventy-two returned with joy and said, "Lord, even the demons submit to us in your name." He replied, "I saw Satan fall like lightning from heaven. I have given you authority to trample on snakes and scorpions and to overcome all the power of the enemy; nothing will harm you."
>
> Luke 10:17–19 (NASB)

Certainly this was shock and awe to the powers of darkness. First, Jesus sent twelve and then seventy. Satan must have been enraged and all the more frantic to get rid of Jesus before He gave this ability to more humans. He probably feared that this was how Jesus planned to reestablish His dominion on the Holy Mountain and even on the whole earth. But as previously stated, Jesus did not come the first time to retake His Mountain by force. Rather, He came to offer Himself as a sacrifice atop the ancient Mountain. When the seventy came back expressing their joy, Jesus gave a short prophecy about Satan being cast out of heaven at the start of the three-and-a-half-year great tribulation. These were words of war, adding insult to injury. Satan is going to fall from heaven like lightning, indicating the force with which he will be ejected from heaven and the destructive wrath he will bring upon the earth as a result, which is the seventh trumpet plague as covered in the chapter "Seven Trumpets and Three Woes" of volume 1. The disciples were given authority to trample the powers of darkness. All the more foreboding was that the disciples were protected from the enemy being able to harm them in return. Again, this was even before they had been given the Holy Spirit. The only weapon they had was the mighty name of Jesus. Little did Satan know that God was preparing for a new phase in the war for dominion that exploits the decisive victory of the cross and the resurrection. Sometime later after the sending forth of the seventy, Jesus gave another prophecy that must have left Satan paranoid.

> And I also say to you that you are Peter, and upon this rock I will build My church; and the gates of Hades shall not overpower it. I will give you the keys of the kingdom of heaven; and whatever you shall bind on earth shall be bound in heaven, and whatever you shall loose on earth shall be loosed in heaven.
>
> Matthew 16:18–19 (NASB)

The presence of the church has had a binding or restraining affect on the satanic forces in this world. Satan has not been able to prevail against this hindrance. Jesus did not reveal at that time how the church would have such power. But it all became clearer at the time of the ascension. Just before Jesus ascended to heaven He gave a promise to the disciples that Satan certainly hated to hear.

> But you shall receive power when the Holy Spirit has come upon you; and you shall be My witnesses both in Jerusalem, and in all Judea and Samaria, and even to the remotest part of the earth.
>
> Acts 1:8 (NASB)

Satan has long been acquainted with the person and the power of the Holy Spirit in human history. Jesus promised these humans that every one of them were going to be empowered by the Holy Spirit to take the gospel to all the nations that are in the possession of Satan—nations that he seeks desperately to unite under one evil ruler and one depraved religion in order to bring the entire world into subjection to himself. How can he prevail with humans empowered by the omnipotent Spirit of God standing in his way? Jesus said the gates of Hades shall not overpower the church, Matthew 16:18. The day that the Holy Spirit was poured out on the disciples of Christ must have been a grim day for Satan.

> And when the day of Pentecost had come, they were all together in one place. And suddenly there came from heaven a noise like a violent, rushing wind, and it filled the whole house where they were sitting. And there appeared to them tongues as of fire distributing themselves, and they rested on each one of them. And they were all filled with the Holy Spirit and began to speak with other tongues, as the Spirit was giving them utterance. Now there were Jews living in Jerusalem, devout men, from every nation under heaven. And when this sound occurred, the multitude came together, and were bewildered, because they were each one hearing them speak in his own language.
>
> Acts 2:1–6 (NASB)

Satan had been plotting and working and killing for centuries trying to overcome the language barrier and national boundaries that God established at the Tower of Babel. It had been a continual hindrance to him. Suddenly the Holy Spirit arrived and gave the disciples supernatural ability to communicate in the languages of all who were present. What Satan had been trying to accomplish through centuries of violence, the Holy Spirit miraculously accomplished with little effort. The disciples did not even have to threaten or kill anyone to make them understand. All those present were astounded that they could understand what these Galileans were saying. What had to be even more irksome to Satan was the message the disciples were communicating, that Jesus was the promised Messiah and that He was raised from the dead. The day of Pentecost started the first phase of God's plan for the church, which was the evangelism of Jerusalem and all Judea.

Then the next step came just as Jesus had instructed. The gospel and the Holy Spirit went to the Samaritans, and the satanic forces had no power to stop it.

> Now when the apostles in Jerusalem heard that Samaria had received the word of God, they sent them Peter and John, who came down and prayed for them, that they might receive the Holy Spirit. For He had not yet fallen upon any of them; they had simply been baptized in the name of the Lord Jesus. Then they began laying their hands on them, and they were receiving the Holy Spirit.
>
> Acts 8:14–17 (NASB)

The biggest shock to the satanic forces, however, must have come when the gospel and the power and indwelling of the Holy Spirit were given to gentiles, the nations and peoples that had long been the possession of Satan. God miraculously arranged a meeting between Peter and a Roman centurion named Cornelius.

Peter had a bit of consternation over God's command to go to the house of an unclean gentile. But realizing that God was in control, he communicated the gospel of Jesus Christ to Cornelius and his household.

> "Of Him all the prophets bear witness that through His name everyone who believes in Him receives forgiveness of sins." While Peter was still speaking these words, the Holy Spirit fell upon all those who were listening to the message. And all the circumcised believers who had come with Peter were amazed, because the gift of the Holy Spirit had been poured out upon the Gentiles also. For they were hearing them speaking with tongues and exalting God. Then Peter answered, "Surely no one can refuse the water for these to be baptized who have received the Holy Spirit just as we did, can he?"
>
> Acts 10:43–47 (NASB)

If the circumcised Jews who were with Peter were amazed, certainly Satan shuddered. There was no need for the gentiles to be circumcised or go to the temple to keep the feasts. All that was needed was faith in Jesus Christ, and God poured out the powerful Holy Spirit on them free of charge. The gentiles were even speaking in different languages to enable them to take the gospel to other gentiles. The display of speaking in tongues by Cornelius and his family was the authentication to the Jews that the indwelling power of the Holy Spirit had been given to the gentiles, just as the Jews had received on the day of Pentecost. In the war for dominion, however, this manifestation in the gentiles had an even more significant purpose. There were many ways God could have given a sign that the Holy Spirit had been given to the gentiles, but God chose the sign of speaking in tongues. The primary reason is because this was the supernatural gift that Satan feared the most. From the day of Pentecost, the purpose of the gift of tongues was to enable rapid implementation of God's mandate to "go therefore and make disciples of all the nations" (Matthew 28:19, NASB). There was no need for the disciples of Christ to take time to learn the languages of the nations. Through this supernatural gift the gospel spread quickly from Jerusalem just as Jesus had commanded, to the peoples of the nations that Satan claimed to be under his control.

> But you shall receive power when the Holy Spirit has come upon you; and you shall be My witnesses both in Jerusalem, and in all Judea and Samaria, and even to the remotest part of the earth.
>
> Acts 1:8 (NASB)

Through the gift of tongues God began the process of building a worldwide holy nation made up of people from all the nations on earth, 1 Peter 2:9–10. This is an even bigger miracle than God forging the nation Israel in the midst of the nation Egypt, Deuteronomy 4:34.

It is no wonder that Satan worked to distract the early church from the purpose of the spiritual gift of tongues. Those with this awesome ability became haughty and used their gifts purely for the purpose of making a spectacle of themselves. This was a problem most evident in the church at Corinth. They became imitators of Satan by using the awesome ability given to them to serve themselves, just as Lucifer abused the many blessings given to him to serve himself.

> For who regards you as superior? And what do you have that you did not receive? But if you did receive it, why do you boast as if you had not received it?
>
> 1 Corinthians 4:7 (NASB)

People were supposed to be drawn into the church through this miraculous gift, but because of inappropriate use of the gift and pseudo-displays that were unbiblical, people outside the church thought it was a club for the insane and wanted nothing to do with the church.

> So then tongues are for a sign, not to those who believe, but to unbelievers; but prophecy is for a sign, not to unbelievers, but to those who believe. If therefore the whole church should assemble together and all speak in tongues, and ungifted men or unbelievers enter, will they not say that you are mad?
>
> 1 Corinthians 14:22–23 (NASB)

The reputation of the church was getting so bad that churches started forbidding the function of the gift of tongues. By neutralizing the gift of tongues, Satan was achieving his goal to stop the spreading of the gospel to many nations. But Paul knew that this gift was vital to the outreach of the church into the nations of the earth.

> Therefore, my brethren, desire earnestly to prophesy, and do not forbid to speak in tongues. But let all things be done properly and in an orderly manner.
>
> 1 Corinthians 14:39–40 (NASB)

Instead of prohibiting the use of the gift, Paul demanded that the gift of speaking in languages be used only for the purpose that God intended. God's design was to give the church this supernatural ability to work around the language barrier Satan has continually struggled to overcome.

Even though the enemy brought his many attacks against the church, the good news of Jesus Christ successfully spread to the nations of the earth as people of every language were delivered out of Satan's kingdom of darkness. The church, empowered by the Holy Spirit, has continued to stand as another obstacle to Satan in his ongoing effort to bring the whole world under his total dominion. Destroying the church from the earth would not be a matter of removing one nation or one race of people but would require Satan to remove people of many races and nations. It is the reverse of the parable of the Wheat and the Tares, Matthew 13:24–30. The church is the wheat planted among Satan's tares. To remove the wheat, Satan would have to remove his tares also.

The passages about the reward of becoming eternal royal priests were covered briefly in the previous chapter of this book. This is a marvelous eternal status that every believer has the potential of receiving. At the beginning of Revelation, John writes about the marvelous place Jesus Christ has secured for us in the plan of God.

> John to the seven churches that are in Asia: Grace to you and peace, from Him who is and who was and who is to come; and from the seven Spirits who are before His throne; and from Jesus Christ, the faithful witness, the first-born of the dead, and the ruler of the kings of the earth. To Him who loves us, and released us from our sins by His blood, and He has made us to be a kingdom, priests to His God and Father; to Him be the glory and the dominion forever and ever. Amen.
>
> Revelation 1:4–6 (NASB)

Revelation is addressed "to the seven churches of Asia" from Jesus Christ who "has made us to be a kingdom, priests to His God and Father." John uses the word *us*, meaning that he includes himself and the believers in the seven churches as those whom God desires to make priests in the coming kingdom. *Us* also includes all the faithful believers throughout church history. "His blood" was the high price Jesus Christ paid for us to have this honored position. This act of Jesus Christ will be the cause for the outbreak of great praise of Him by the entire holy angelic heavenly host.

> And when He had taken the book, the four living creatures and the twenty-four elders fell down before the Lamb, having each one a harp, and golden bowls full of incense, which are the prayers of the saints. And they sang a new song, saying, "Worthy art Thou to take the book, and to break its seals; for Thou wast slain, and didst purchase for God with Thy blood men from every tribe and tongue and people and nation. And Thou hast made them to be a kingdom and priests to our God; and they will reign upon the earth." And I looked, and I heard the voice of many angels around the throne and the living creatures and the elders; and the number of them was myriads of myriads, and thousands of thousands, saying with a loud voice, "Worthy is the Lamb that was slain to receive power and riches and wisdom and might and honor and glory and blessing."
>
> Revelation 5:8–12 (NASB)

The heavenly host will praise the Lamb as being worthy to open the seven-seal scroll because it is by His blood that He has cleared the way for people of all languages to become priests to God. This song is referring to faithful believers from every period of human history, including the church age. The church has been comprised of peoples from many nations and languages since the day of Pentecost, Acts 2:6–12 and 37–41. If the sacrifice made by Jesus Christ to make us "a kingdom and priests" for God is the cause for such great overwhelming praise of the Lamb by all the heavenly host, then it certainly ought to be cause for believers to be continually mindful of and to exploit this blessed once-in-eternity opportunity. This should be cause for all the church to join now the angelic host in worshipping and singing praises to the Lamb.

Peter also writes about this awesome achievement that Jesus Christ accomplishes for His church and through His church in the war for dominion.

> But you are a chosen race, a royal priesthood, a holy nation, a people for God's own possession, that you may proclaim the excellencies of Him who has called you out of darkness into His marvelous light; for you once were not a people, but now you are the people of God; you had not received mercy, but now you have received mercy.
>
> 1 Peter 2:9–10 (NASB)

In this passage, Peter is quoting the words that God had spoken to Israel at Mt. Sinai shortly after He had delivered them out of Egypt.

> "'Now then, if you will indeed obey My voice and keep My covenant, then you shall be My own possession among all the peoples, for all the earth is Mine; and you shall be to Me a kingdom of priests and a holy nation.' These are the words that you shall speak to the sons of Israel."
>
> Exodus 19:5–6 (NASB)

The first thing to notice in this passage is the conditional statement from God, "if you will indeed obey My voice and keep My covenant." Being eternally included in the kingdom of priests and the holy nation has always been conditional. There was a temporal and an eternal aspect of this communication that God made to Moses and Israel at Mt. Sinai. The temporal desire of God was that Israel represent Him to the rest of the nations of earth that were under Satan's control. All the rest of the human race at that time worshipped Satan through their pagan idols.

The eternal desire of God is that Israel be included in the eternal royal priesthood. The third day after God spoke these words to Moses, God came down on Mt. Sinai and spoke the Ten Commandments to all Israel for all to hear, Exodus 19:10–20:17. The holy presence of God and the sound of His voice caused the people of Israel great fear, Exodus 20:18–20. This was God's intention, that the people fear sinning against Him, especially the sin of idolatry, which is the worship of Satan. However, this ominous impression was not long lasting in the minds of the people of Israel. It was not long after this that the golden calf worship incident occurred while Moses was on Mt. Sinai getting the tablets of stone with the Ten Commandments written on them. Due to Israel's rebellion, God has not yet been able to make Israel to be the kingdom of priests on the earth in the temporal realm as He has desired them to be. However, God still has a plan that His chosen people will yet become a holy nation and priests to represent Him to the nations on the earth. Sovereign God will accomplish this for Israel in the coming kingdom of Christ, Isaiah 61:6. Throughout the history of Israel there have been many of God's chosen people who have been obedient and will have the eternal reward of being royal eternal priests. In order for any believer to become an eternal royal priest, it is necessary to succeed in being a priest in the temporal realm.

The letter in which Peter quotes these words was written to Jewish believers in the early church who had been dispersed out of Israel and among the gentile nations, 1 Peter 1:1–2. The reason Peter addresses the letter to dispersed Jewish believers is because he was the apostle to the circumcised and Paul was the apostle to the uncircumcised, Galatians 2:7–8. That is not to say that Peter's letters are only for Jews in the church. Most Bible scholars agree that Peter wrote this letter a few years after Paul wrote his letter to the church at Ephesus, in which he revealed the mystery of this age that both Jews and gentiles are joined together in one body, Ephesians 2:11–3:10. It is not logical that Peter would have written a letter specific to Jews in the church after Paul had clearly stated that believers from the gentile nations have equal status with the Jews in the church. Therefore the opportunity and means for all believers in the church to become eternal royal priests is the same. It is necessary to succeed as a priest in the temporal realm first.

If God has been unsuccessful to this point in time of making one race of people, Israel, into priests on the earth in the temporal realm, one might ask, how can He accomplish it with peoples of many nations that make up the church? Only by the power of God the Holy Spirit can such a miracle be performed. Since the church is made up of peoples of many nations it has much broader impact than what could have been achieved through the one nation, Israel. The fact that there have been peoples of every tribe, tongue, and nation united as priests on the earth throughout the time of the church is a very significant victory in the war for dominion. Satan has long tried to unite people of the nations into one evil entity, and he has continually failed. But through the body of Jesus Christ on earth, God has succeeded in uniting people from every language into "a holy nation" that transcends national boundaries.

The church present on the earth today can be and should be living as a holy nation now and a kingdom of priests now. Eternal life begins at the point of salvation through faith in the death and resurrection of Jesus Christ. As with Israel, some believers in the church will be faithful and others will fail. Just prior to Peter writing to the church about being royal priests and a holy nation in 1 Peter 2:9–10, he reveals the way believers are to function as priests in the temporal life.

> [11]Therefore, putting aside all malice and all deceit and hypocrisy and envy and all slander, [2]like newborn babies, long for the pure milk of the word, so that by it you may grow in respect to salvation, [3]if you have tasted the kindness of the Lord.

> ⁴And coming to Him as to a living stone which has
> been rejected by men, but is choice and precious in the
> sight of God, ⁵you also, as living stones, are being built
> up as a spiritual house for a holy priesthood, to offer up
> spiritual sacrifices acceptable to God through Jesus Christ.
>
> 1 Peter 2:1–5 (NASB)

As priests in this temporal life, believers are to put away sin. In verse 1, Peter lists sins that can be especially problematic in local churches. As indicated in other chapters of this book, this is not a call to sinless perfection in the temporal life. However, a momentum of growing in God's Word and walking in the power of the Holy Spirit is essential. In verse 2, Peter states that the priest is to long for the Word of God as babies long for and need milk. The Word causes growth so as to become more and more effective as a priest. The priest also comes to experience more and more of the Lord's kindness (verse 3). God is then able to use the priest as a living stone to build up a spiritual house for the priesthood (verse 4). The faithful believers are the living stones that make up the holy house and they are the priests who do ministry in the holy house (verse 5). Each priest is to make a sacrifice in the holy house, and the sacrifice that is to be offered is one's self. These are the actions required for a believer to successfully function as a priest in the temporal realm. God views believers who are faithful to these commands as choice and precious living stones.

In 1 Peter 2:10, Peter wrote, "For you once were not a people, but now you are a people of God" (NASB). From our natural births we are not a people acceptable to God because we are fallen in sin. At salvation we become a people of God's own possession, and He gives us citizenship in a holy nation on earth that has no association with national and racial human boundaries. Each believer will choose whether to live in the reality of being a citizen of the holy nation. All boundaries that divide the human race are overcome in Christ. Believers who live as citizens of the holy nation will not be so influenced by those barriers.

> For all of you who were baptized into Christ have clothed yourselves with Christ. There is neither Jew nor Greek, there is neither slave nor free man, there is neither male nor female; for you are all one in Christ Jesus. And if you belong to Christ, then you are Abraham's offspring, heirs according to promise.
>
> Galatians 3:27–29 (NASB)

The nation Israel is the physical offspring of Abraham that God desires to be a holy nation and priests on the earth. The church is the spiritual offspring of Abraham as children of faith, Romans 4:16. God desires all who are in the church to be a holy nation and priests on the earth though it is made up of people of many races, levels of social status, and both genders. Obviously, Paul is not communicating that believers all become the same gender and race and have equal social status as a result of salvation. God is the Creator of these human diversities and He does not change these traits when a person places their faith in Jesus Christ. God made the humans male and female to create the gender barrier. A woman is not to function as a man, and a man is not to function as a woman. God created all the races so there are many racial barriers. God separated the human race into the different languages at the Tower of Babel to establish the language barrier. God gives and withholds worldly prosperity, which gives each person their social status. The diversities of race, social status, and gender are all boundaries that result in divisions and conflicts in the human race. God created the barriers, but God does not cause the conflicts that result from the barriers. The conflicts and divisions are due to the human fallen nature. The pride of each person's flesh nature drives these prejudices. No type of human government and no social engineering program of any kind can accomplish unity among all the diversities of the human race. All human attempts to unite humanity will ultimately fail. There have even been attempts by the enemy to overcome the barrier that separates humans from animals so as to view and treat animals as humans and humans as animals. All the barriers that God has ordained stand firm, even as those in nature stand firm, Proverbs 8:29 and Psalm 104:6–9. God ordained and established these barriers, and nobody but God can overcome them. The fleshly relational problems that result from the barriers among the human race become insignificant between members of the body of Christ. However, the animosities along the boundaries of human diversities are not instantly removed at salvation. Freedom from the burdensome human conflicts associated with race, social status, and gender are removed gradually.

> Therefore consider the members of your earthly body as dead to immorality, impurity, passion, evil desire, and greed, which amounts to idolatry. For it is on account of these things that the wrath of God will come, and in them you also once walked, when you were living in them. But now you also, put them all aside: anger, wrath, malice, slander, and abusive speech from your mouth. Do not lie to one another, since you laid aside the old self with its evil practices, and have put on the new self who is being renewed to a true knowledge according to the image of the One who created him—a renewal in which there is no distinction between Greek and Jew, circumcised and uncircumcised, barbarian, Scythian, slave and freeman, but Christ is all, and in all.
>
> Colossians 3:5–11 (NASB)

To overcome the conflicts that result from these human diversities, it is crucial that each member of the body of Christ lays aside their old self and "put on the new self" through the miraculous transformation of God's Word. The laying aside of the old self is accomplished by the Holy Spirit that God the Father has given to live inside every believer in Jesus Christ, Galatians 5:16–17. The same Holy Spirit living inside each of us is also the One who teaches us the Word of God that accomplishes the miraculous transformation into the new self.

> You are a letter of Christ, cared for by us, written not with ink, but with the Spirit of the living God, not on tablets of stone, but on tablets of human hearts.
>
> 2 Corinthians 3:3 (NASB)

> Now we have received, not the spirit of the world, but the Spirit who is from God, that we might know the things freely given to us by God, which things we also speak, not in words taught by human wisdom, but in those taught by the Spirit, combining spiritual thoughts with spiritual words.
>
> 1 Corinthians 2:12–13 (NASB)

> But he who is spiritual appraises all things, yet he himself is appraised by no man. For who has known the mind of the Lord, that he should instruct Him? But we have the mind of Christ.
>
> 1 Corinthians 2:15–16 (NASB)

As believers grow in the Word of God they grow up into the Head of the church, Jesus Christ. Growing into the Head, we all become of the same mind which is the mind of Jesus Christ.

> Until we all attain to the unity of the faith, and of the knowledge of the Son of God, to a mature man, to the measure of the stature which belongs to the fullness of Christ. As a result, we are no longer to be children, tossed here and there by waves, and carried about by every wind of doctrine, by the trickery of men, by craftiness in deceitful

scheming; but speaking the truth in love, we are to grow up in all aspects into Him, who is the head, even Christ, from whom the whole body, being fitted and held together by that which every joint supplies, according to the proper working of each individual part, causes the growth of the body for the building up of itself in love.

Ephesians 4:13–16 (NASB)

This gradual maturing process of believers by the Word of God results in a diversity of new selves who all think with the same mind as the Head, Jesus Christ. This is how the conflicts and prejudices associated with human diversities in the body of Christ are overcome.

Now I exhort you, brethren, by the name of our Lord Jesus Christ, that you all agree, and there be no divisions among you, but you be made complete in the same mind and in the same judgment.

1Corinthians 1:10 (NASB)

If therefore there is any encouragement in Christ, if there is any consolation of love, if there is any fellowship of the Spirit, if any affection and compassion, make my joy complete by being of the same mind, maintaining the same love, united in spirit, intent on one purpose.

Philippians 2:1–2 (NASB)

Conflicts associated with gender, race, social status are removed. Each believer is to be one with believers of every language, every race, every nationality, every social status, every age, and both genders. Thus, there is no basis for divisiveness between believers that is based on prejudices associated with these diversities in the human race. All those designations of diversity are associated with the nature of each human's first birth in the flesh. Believers are going to spend eternity together, so they need to start dealing with each other as though the eternal future is already here.

> Therefore from now on we recognize no man according to the flesh; even though we have known Christ according to the flesh, yet now we know Him thus no longer. Therefore if any man is in Christ, he is a new creature; the old things passed away; behold, new things have come.
>
> 2 Corinthians 5:16–17 (NASB)

There is no reason for a child of God filled with the Holy Spirit to have prejudices based on gender, race, nationality, social status or age. This is especially true if a person of another race or language is a brother or sister in Christ.

> So then, while we have opportunity, let us do good to all men, and especially to those who are of the household of the faith.
>
> Galatians 6:10 (NASB)

In the body of Christ, no man should look down upon his eternal sisters as inferior. Certainly there are duties in the church that God allows only men to perform, 1 Timothy 2:12-15, but the women have the same powerful Holy Spirit living in them as do the men. The women in the church can be mighty servants of God. In the body of Christ, no woman should be resentful toward her eternal brothers, desiring to prove herself superior to men. The new-self man and the new-self woman will be very comfortable and content in the special place that God has ordained for both genders. Believers of one race should never consider believers of another race inferior. Believers of every race have the same all powerful indwelling Holy Spirit. There is no reason why believers with temporal material wealth should consider themselves superior to fellow believers who are poor, 1

Timothy 6:17-19 and James 2:5. Also, believers who have little should never look with envy at fellow believers who are materially blessed, Hebrews 13:5. The new-self believer who is wealthy will have compassion for believers who struggle to succeed and the new-self believer who is poor will rejoice with wealthy believers for their success. This divine love between members of such diversity can only be accomplished in the body of Christ. Neither man nor Satan can achieve such miracles of unity.

These things are the ideal, and certainly the church has never fully realized the unity of love that comes from the Holy Spirit. But as always, the success of God's plan is not dependent on the success or failure of any created being. God is sovereign, and He is able to accomplish His plan, though the church is full of frail beings prone to walk in the flesh. This reality is proven when believers of one church work in harmony with believers of another church who differ in their doctrinal stands. Because of the fruit of the Holy Spirit, those who are saved through faith in Jesus Christ are able to work together in the common goal of representing Jesus Christ on the earth, even if their theology differs. Being able to accept differences is very much a part of love, and doing so in the power of the Spirit does not compromise one's theological position. The only exception to this would be if a group is teaching a different gospel for salvation or is condoning immorality in obvious violation of God's law. Those who are growing together in God's Word, being renewed in their minds, are powerful, being transformed into new beings who are the very character image of God on the inside.

> That, in reference to your former manner of life, you lay aside the old self, which is being corrupted in accordance with the lusts of deceit, and that you be renewed in the spirit of your mind, and put on the new self, which in the likeness of God has been created in righteousness and holiness of the truth.
>
> Ephesians 4:22–24 (NASB)

The makeover into the "new self" is available to every believer by being "renewed to a true knowledge of the One who created him," regardless of the believer's background. It can happen in every believer, and every believer desperately needs it. The impact of the whole church on the kingdom of darkness would be much greater if more believers became miraculously transformed to the new self by the renewing of their minds. Imagine the witness the church would have if all the barriers and distinctions that exist between members of the human race were fully overcome in the worldwide body of Christ. Unfortunately, many believers miss out on this progressive transformation because they refuse to feed their minds on God's Word. It is only the new self, not the old self, who is able to work in unity with the rest of the whole body of Christ. The daily intake of truth is the only way the new self is strengthened and united with the rest of the body, being connected to Jesus Christ, the head.

As covered earlier in this chapter, we are to be priests to God through the blood of Jesus Christ. All the heavenly host sings out praises to the Lamb for this great accomplishment. Under the Mosaic law, the duty of the priests was to perform the ritual sacrifices for the people of Israel and the nation as a whole. The priests were the only ones authorized by God to enter the holy of holies to empty out the blood on the mercy seat, Leviticus 16:29–34. In this age all believers in Jesus Christ have direct access right now in this temporal life into the heavenly holy of holies as priests.

> Since therefore, brethren, we have confidence to enter the holy place by the blood of Jesus, by a new and living way which He inaugurated for us through the veil, that is, His flesh, and since we have a great priest over the house of God, let us draw near with a sincere heart in full assurance of faith, having our hearts sprinkled clean from an evil conscience and our bodies washed with pure water.
>
> Hebrews 10:19–22 (NASB)

But when Christ appeared as a high priest of the good things to come, He entered through the greater and more perfect tabernacle, not made with hands, that is to say, not of this creation; and not through the blood of goats and calves, but through His own blood, He entered the holy place once for all, having obtained eternal redemption.

Hebrews 9:11–12 (NASB)

Since Jesus Christ has inaugurated the way for us through the veil, every royal priest is able to go with full assurance before the throne of our heavenly Father anytime and from anyplace on earth. Like the priests of Israel, so also believer priests of the church are to make a sacrifice to the Lord. The sacrifice we are to offer is ourselves, as Jesus offered Himself as a sacrifice.

I urge you therefore, brethren, by the mercies of God, to present your bodies a living and holy sacrifice, acceptable to God, which is your spiritual service of worship. And do not be conformed to this world, but be transformed by the renewing of your mind, that you may prove what the will of God is, that which is good and acceptable and perfect.

Romans 12:1–2 (NASB)

The "living and holy sacrifice" is each believer putting to death or laying aside their flesh natures by the power of the Holy Spirit. Believers who make this sacrifice gain a supernatural peace and joy and stability in life. This sacrifice is a spiritual service of worship that is acceptable to God. When believers sacrifice their old selves, they are being imitators of Christ, who inaugurated the way for us into the heavenly holy of holies by His own precious blood. In addition to giving ourselves as sacrifices, our priestly duties also include the renewing of our minds by the power of God's Word and the Holy Spirit.

> But an hour is coming, and now is, when the true worshipers shall worship the Father in spirit and truth; for such people the Father seeks to be His worshipers. God is spirit, and those who worship Him must worship in spirit and truth.
>
> John 4:23–24 (NASB)

This prophecy of Jesus, worshiping God in spirit and truth, started being fulfilled on the day of Pentecost. Believers have no need to travel to a temple building on earth. Believers are the temple wherever they go and the worship of God by the Spirit and the truth is to be continually taking place from the temple.

As the King of Kings, Jesus Christ is coming to displace Satan who is currently the ruler of this world, John 12:31. The bride of Christ is coming to displace the fallen angelic powers of wickedness who currently rule with Satan on this earth, Ephesians 6:12. Satan and his fallen angels do not want to be displaced by beings made from the dust of the ground, so they struggle against the church, especially those who are the obedient believers who will form the bride of Christ.

> For our struggle is not against flesh and blood, but against the rulers, against the powers, against the world forces of this darkness, against the spiritual forces of wickedness in the heavenly places.
>
> Ephesians 6:12 (NASB)

The rulers, powers, and forces are the hierarchy of fallen angelic authorities through whom Satan exercises authority over the nations. The church is steeped in the battle for dominion. Any believer who would desire to ignore the battle is already a casualty. The believer's life after salvation is the only opportunity that believer has for all eternity to glorify God in this war. God has graciously provided us the power, the authority and weapons to stand against a most vicious enemy.

Therefore, take up the full armor of God, so that you will be able to resist in the evil day, and having done everything, to stand firm. Stand firm therefore, HAVING GIRDED YOUR LOINS WITH TRUTH, and HAVING PUT ON THE BREASTPLATE OF RIGHTEOUSNESS, and having shod YOUR FEET WITH THE PREPARATION OF THE GOSPEL OF PEACE; in addition to all, taking up the shield of faith with which you will be able to extinguish all the flaming arrows of the evil one. And take THE HELMET OF SALVATION, and the sword of the Spirit, which is the word of God. With all prayer and petition pray at all times in the Spirit, and with this in view, be on the alert with all perseverance and petition for all the saints,

Ephesians 6:13–18 (NASB)

Paul also refers to the armor of God as the "armor of light" in Romans 13:12–14, where Paul associates putting on the armor with putting away the deeds of the flesh. Wearing the armor of God and walking in the flesh are diametrically opposed conditions. The more time believers spend dressed in the armor, the more effective they become as warriors against the unseen forces of darkness. Believers who spend more time living in the flesh will not be effective as warriors, but will be casualties. In verse 13 and 14, Paul directs believers to do everything to stand firm. Believers are not to flee in fear from the unseen enemy, but rather stand firm in the strength of the Lord against the enemy.

Finally, be strong in the Lord and in the strength of His might. Put on the full armor of God, so that you will be able to stand firm against the schemes of the devil.

Ephesians 6:10–11 (NASB)

We are to be on the alert regarding our adversary the devil, 1 Peter 5:8, but nowhere in Scripture does God tell believers to fear Satan. In Revelation 2:10 the church at Smyrna is told "do not fear" what the devil was about to do, casting some of them into prison. Believers who are weak because they live in the flesh will be afraid and will desert their posts attempting to escape this ruthless and desperate enemy. The only way to deal with the bully is to stand firm against him in the power of the omnipotent Holy Spirit whom God has given to indwell every believer. "Having done everything to stand firm" includes confession and repentance of sin, abiding daily in the Word of God, being continually filled with the Holy Spirit and being in persistent prayer.

In the same letter to the Ephesians that Paul teaches about the armor of God, he also reveals to every member of the body of Christ that they are positionally seated in the place of authority in heaven.

> Even when we were dead in our transgressions, made us alive together with Christ (by grace you have been saved), and raised us up with Him, and seated us with Him in the heavenly places, in Christ Jesus.
>
> Ephesians 2:5–6 (NASB)

> For by grace you have been saved through faith; and that not of yourselves, it is the gift of God.
>
> Ephesians 2:8 (NASB)

Every believer is elevated to this place of authority at the moment of salvation. Like salvation, this authority is given by the grace of God to everyone who believes. Prior to this verse, Paul reveals that in the heavenly places Jesus Christ has authority over all the powers of darkness.

> These are in accordance with the working of the strength of His might which He brought about in Christ, when He raised Him from the dead, and seated Him at His

right hand in the heavenly places, far above all rule and authority and power and dominion, and every name that is named, not only in this age, but also in the one to come. And He put all things in subjection under His feet, and gave Him as head over all things to the church, which is His body, the fullness of Him who fills all in all.

Ephesians 1:19–23 (NASB)

The authority of Jesus Christ flows from His heavenly seat, through the body of Christ against the satanic forces. That is the reason the body of Christ, the church, is seated there with Him. God would not command the church in this same Ephesians letter to take up the full armor of God to battle the powers of darkness if He did not also give the church the place of power and authority to do so. In Jesus Christ, every believer is elevated to a position not given to any of the angelic host.

When He had made purification of sins, He sat down at the right hand of the Majesty on high; having become as much better than the angels, as He has inherited a more excellent name than they.

Hebrews 1:3–4 (NASB)

But to which of the angels has He ever said, "Sit at My right hand, until I make Thine enemies a footstool for Thy feet"?

Hebrews 1:13 (NASB)

This passage is a rebuttal to Satan and the fallen angelic host who seek the place of supreme power. Every believer in Jesus Christ is seated in the most coveted place of power and authority. Being positionally seated at the right hand of the heavenly Father, every Christian has the authority to command the fallen satanic angelic powers. Not even the mightiest of the holy angelic host give such commands to the fallen angelic realm.

Yet in the same manner these men, also by dreaming, defile the flesh, and reject authority, and revile angelic majesties. But Michael the archangel, when he disputed with the devil and argued about the body of Moses, did not dare pronounce against him a railing judgment, but said, "The Lord rebuke you."

Jude 8–9 (NASB)

These men who "defile the flesh, and reject authority, and revile angelic majesties" are people empowered by demonic forces. Their condition is a consequence of indulging in the corrupt desires of the flesh.

[10]And especially those who indulge the flesh in its corrupt desires and despise authority. [11]Daring, self-willed, they do not tremble when they revile angelic majesties, whereas angels who are greater in might and power do not bring a reviling judgment against them before the Lord.

2 Peter 2:10–11 (NASB)

Under the influence of the evil ones, they rail against the holy heavenly host just as the beast will do when he is empowered by Satan, Revelation 13:5–6. This is Satan's counterfeit to the authority given to the saints of the Lord in the church.

God wants believers to utilize the authority they have in Jesus Christ through daily spiritual warfare prayers. Paul makes it very clear that prayer is a vital part of the battle as he commands in Ephesians 6:18, "With all prayer and petition pray at all times in the Spirit…be on the alert with all perseverance and petition for all the saints" (NASB). Believers faithful to their calling in Christ, living as new spiritual creations by the power of the Holy Spirit, can legitimately take authority over the unseen satanic forces and come against them in the mighty name of Jesus Christ. This has to be an act of faith in the filling of the Holy Spirit for there to be discernment and power in the exercise of this authority. Unfaithful believers lack the confidence that they have such authority, and their weak faith denies that such action will have any effect. Believers living faithfully to Jesus Christ, however, will be bold and confident in their prayers of spiritual warfare on behalf of their fellow saints. God will often allow them to see the impact of their prayers. But even when there is no visible evidence that the enemy is being impacted, believers need to have faith that the world forces of darkness are suffering and being tormented as a result. The fallen angelic realm is desperate, and they are determined to fight on even if they are in agony. Satan and his evil forces are very leery of the power and authority the church possesses through the indwelling Holy Spirit. The satanic powers use various schemes to stop believers from wielding the power and authority given to them. One of their ploys is to draw believers away from God.

> Submit therefore to God. Resist the devil and he will flee from you. Draw near to God and He will draw near to you. cleanse your hands, you sinners; and purify your hearts, you double-minded.
>
> James 4:7–8 (NASB)

Satan wants to lure believers away from being close to God. The devil knows believers with dirty hands and impure hearts will not be able to exercise the authority over his worldly powers of darkness as God has intended them to do. Believers who are continually walking in the flesh are weak and most ineffective in trying to wield the heavenly power. Another ploy Satan uses is to deceive believers into thinking they have no such authority. When the commander of a military realizes his enemy has an ultimate weapon more powerful than any of his weapons, that commander works to keep his enemy from using that ultimate weapon. The evil commander has masterfully worked to convince the church that the power of the Holy Spirit is ineffective, or that it does not exist at all. Those who lead Christians in the deception that believers have no authority over the power of darkness are doing a great service for the enemy. The satanic powers are probably most grateful. Satan has distracted the church from the reality of this power because he knows that if the whole church were to believe and practice this truth, the forces of darkness would be overwhelmed. The Holy Spirit is more than an equalizer for every member of the body of Christ.

> You are from God, little children, and have overcome them; because greater is He who is in you than he who is in the world.
>
> 1 John 4:4 (NASB)

But the truth of God's Word reveals that believers of the church do have power to command the demonic powers.

> And she continued doing this for many days. But Paul was greatly annoyed, and turned and said to the spirit, "I command you in the name of Jesus Christ to come out of her!" And it came out at that very moment.
>
> Acts 16:18 (NASB)

> And the seventy returned with joy, saying, "Lord, even the demons are subject to us in Your name."
>
> Luke 10:17 (NASB)

> Do you not know that we shall judge angels? How much more, matters of this life?
>
> 1 Corinthians 6:3 (NASB)

The beings made lower than angels have been raised up in Christ to a position higher than even the mightiest of the fallen angelic host. That includes all rule and authority and power and dominion, and every name that is named among those who make up the fallen angelic host, not only in this age, but also in the one to come. Believers don't have to be apostles to engage the enemy in battle. The commands of Ephesians 6:10–18 are given to all the church. Any believer living faithfully to the Lord and in the filling of the Holy Spirit can effectively issue verbal commands to the powers of darkness, as a result of the authority they have being seated with Christ. The spiritual warfare prayers of believers walking in the obedience of faith have great impact, James 5:16. Jesus revealed some very important truths about battling the spiritual forces when praying about human relationships.

> "Truly I say to you, whatever you bind on earth shall have been bound in heaven; and whatever you loose on earth shall have been loosed in heaven. "Again I say to you, that if two of you agree on earth about anything that they may ask, it shall be done for them by My Father who is in heaven. "For where two or three have gathered together in My name, I am there in their midst."
>
> Matthew 18:18–20 (NASB)

Binding and loosening is regarding the powers of darkness. Believers who are living in the power and authority of being seated with Christ can bind the evil spiritual forces so that their function is limited, or even stifled. This is especially effective if two or more believers are in agreement when exercising this authority in prayer. The devil is often the real enemy in the midst of what seems to be human conflicts, Ephesians 6:12. While in the privacy of their prayer closet, Christians should not be shy or hesitant about verbally taking authority over and binding and rebuking and commanding the forces of wickedness they sense are operating in their local church and the lives of their families and friends. Fasting is oftentimes an important act when battling against the powers of darkness through prayer, Matthew 17:19–21.

Such prayers are also effective in praying for those who are unsaved. In 2 Corinthians 4:3–4, Paul reveals that the "god of this world," Satan, "has blinded the minds of the unbelieving so that they might not see the light of the gospel of the glory of Christ." Jesus gave a very interesting insight about this when the Pharisees accused Him of casting out demons by Beelzebul.

> Or how can anyone enter the strong man's house and carry off his property, unless he first binds the strong man? And then he will plunder his house. He who is not with Me is against Me; and he who does not gather with Me scatters.
>
> Matthew 12:29–30 (NASB)

Satan is the strong man. The property of the strong man is unsaved humans. Binding the fallen angelic beings working to keep unbelievers blind can force the enemy to stand back so unbelievers can comprehend the truth of the gospel. This is not to say that such action will always result in unbelievers accepting the gospel, but at least they won't be hindered from comprehending to truth. Jesus told His disciples that the powers of darkness will not hinder the church from the mission of bringing the message of salvation to those who in the strong man's house and under his control.

> "I also say to you that you are Peter, and upon this rock I will build My church; and the gates of Hades will not overpower it. I will give you the keys of the kingdom of heaven; and whatever you bind on earth shall have been bound in heaven, and whatever you loose on earth shall have been loosed in heaven."
>
> Matthew 6:18–19 (NASB)

The "gates of Hades" is the same as the strong man's house. The gates are defensive to protect the possessions in the house of the strong man. The "keys of the kingdom" is referring to the gospel which opens the way for unbelievers to escape the house of the strong man and into eternal life. Again, Jesus refers to binding and loosing. Binding the strong man can result in unbelievers being loosed from the strong man's kingdom of darkness. Living ever mindful of the place we have being seated with Jesus Christ is very much a part of our connection to and having a personal relationship with our Lord. There is no fallen angelic power that is immune from believers with a persistent walk in the obedience in faith. Every believer is seated with Christ "far above all" rule and authority and power and dominion and every name that is named "in this age," Ephesians 1:21. The child of God walking in obedience is given abounding power from the throne of Jesus Christ but needs to be vigilantly on guard as the satanic forces work relentlessly to counterattack and to distract the children of God to cause them to walk in disobedience and render them powerless.

Some of the most destructive counterattacks happen when the powers of darkness have access to the minds of believers when they fail to be suited in the armor of light. Here are two biblical examples.

> Then Satan stood up against Israel and moved David to number Israel. God was displeased with this thing, so He struck Israel.
>
> 1 Chronicles 21:1 and 7 (NASB)

> But a man named Ananias, with his wife Sapphira, sold a piece of property, and kept back some of the price for himself, with his wife's full knowledge, and bringing a portion of it, he laid it at the apostles' feet. But Peter said, "Ananias, why has Satan filled your heart to lie to the Holy Spirit and to keep back *some* of the price of the land?
>
> Acts 5:1–3 (NASB)

In these two instances, Satan brought his attacks by manipulating the thoughts of unsuspecting believers as they were not being vigilant of their spiritual conditions. In both cases, the victims were living according to their flesh natures. David wanted to find out how strong Israel was militarily, not recognizing that he was relying on man and not God for protection of the nation. Ananias and Sapphira wanted to put on the illusion that they were in accord with others in the church who had unselfishly sold their properties and gave all the proceeds to the Jerusalem church, Acts 4:32–37. These were seemingly benign acts that Satan exploited to bring his destructive attacks against Israel and against the church. Other fleshly situations that Satan can exploit include anger, Ephesians 4:26-27, and failure to forgive, 2 Corinthians 2:10-11, and depriving one's spouse of intimacy, 1 Corinthians 7:4-5. There are certainly many other human fleshly conditions besides these that the enemy will use to bring counter attacks. Seeing these examples in Scripture should make believers be all the more diligent to follow the example of the Apostle Paul.

> For though we walk in the flesh, we do not war according to the flesh, for the weapons of our warfare are not of the flesh, but divinely powerful for the destruction of fortresses. We are destroying speculations and every lofty thing raised up against the knowledge of God, and we are taking every thought captive to the obedience of Christ, and we are ready to punish all disobedience, whenever your obedience is complete.
>
> 2 Corinthians 10:3–6 (NASB)

When believers are arrayed in the armor of light, they are vigilant by the Holy Spirit to recognize thoughts coming into their minds that are ungodly and reject those thoughts as fleshly or satanic. This is the purpose of the "shield of faith with which you will be able to extinguish all the flaming missiles of the evil one." The flaming missiles are aimed right at believers' minds. These truths should be sobering, but they must not be intimidating nor cause us to fear the powers of darkness. Every believer in this age has the indwelling omnipotent Holy Spirit, who is infinitely more powerful than all the satanic powers combined, 1 John 4:4. Every day is like David facing Goliath for each believer. We must not shy away from confronting the enemy with the faith and confidence of David.

> Then David said to the Philistine, "You come to me with a sword, a spear, and a javelin, but I come to you in the name of the LORD of hosts, the God of the armies of Israel, whom you have taunted.
> and that all this assembly may know that the LORD does not deliver by sword or by spear; for the battle is the LORD's and He will give you into our hands."
>
> 1 Samuel 17:45 and 47 (NASB)

Be warned, this is not for believers living in the weakness of the flesh. As David proclaimed, "the battle is the Lord's." Fleshly believers will fail under the enemy's counter attack. The enemy watches and knows when believers are in the power of Holy Spirit. Believers arrayed in the armor of light have no need to fear the enemy. Satan and the fallen angelic realm want to turn the tables to cause believers to feel intimidated, but in reality, they are the ones who are in fear. They face an omnipotent enemy against whom they cannot win, Who also happens to be our loving Heavenly Father. We have nothing to fear as long as we walk in obedience to our Father. When we fail, the door is open for the enemy to bring his attack of oppression. Psalm 143 is a prayer that David wrote for deliverance from such a spiritual attack after he had fallen in sin.

> Hear my prayer, O Lord, Give ear to my supplications! Answer me in Your faithfulness, in Your righteousness! And do not enter into judgment with Your servant, For in Your sight no man living is righteous. For the enemy has persecuted my soul; He has crushed my life to the ground; He has made me dwell in dark places, like those who have long been dead. Therefore my spirit is overwhelmed within me; My heart is appalled within me.
>
> Psalm 143:1–4 (NASB)

David begins the psalm by confessing his sin that led to the tormented condition of his soul, which is the result of a satanic attack on his mind.

> Deliver me, O LORD, from my enemies; I take refuge in You. Teach me to do Your will, For You are my God; Let Your good Spirit lead me on level ground. For the sake of Your name, O Lord, revive me. In Your righteousness bring my soul out of trouble. And in Your lovingkindness, cut off my enemies and destroy all those who afflict my soul, For I am Your servant.
>
> Psalm 143:9–12 (NASB)

David ends the psalm by asking God to lead him in obedience and to revive him and to destroy the enemy afflicting his soul. David wrote many psalms against his enemies. It is most illuminating to read those psalms from the perspective that he is not writing with regard to flesh and blood enemies: "But against the rulers, against the powers, against the world forces of this darkness, against the spiritual forces of wickedness in the heavenly places" (Ephesians 6:12, NASB). David knew very well the reality of spiritual warfare. David witnessed firsthand the demonic torment that King Saul suffered as a result of his disobedience to God.

Now the Spirit of the Lord departed from Saul, and an evil spirit from the Lord terrorized him.

1 Samuel 16:14 (NASB)

So it came about whenever the *evil* spirit from God came to Saul, David would take the harp and play *it* with his hand; and Saul would be refreshed and be well, and the evil spirit would depart from him.

1 Samuel 16:23 (NASB)

Now it came about on the next day that an evil spirit from God came mightily upon Saul, and he raved in the midst of the house, while David was playing the harp with his hand, as usual; and a spear was in Saul's hand. Saul hurled the spear for he thought, "I will pin David to the wall." But David escaped from his presence twice.

1 Samuel 18:10–11 (NASB)

God intended for David to see the consequences of Saul's sin so that David would be alert and diligent to obey, and to repent when he failed. David wrote Psalm 51 as a repentant prayer after his sin of adultery with Bathsheba and his murder of Uriah the Hittite were exposed by God.

Create in me a clean heart, O God, and renew a steadfast spirit within me. Do not cast me away from Your presence and do not take Your Holy Spirit from me.

Psalm 51:10–11 (NASB)

In his prayer of repentance, David pleads with God to not take His Holy Spirit away from him because he saw what happened to Saul when God removed His Holy Spirit. King Saul expressed repentance for his sin, but it was disingenuous, 1 Samuel 15:20–26. God knows the thoughts and intent of every human heart. In the church age, God does not take away His

Holy Spirit from believers, but there is equally severe divine punishment for wayward believers. There are other examples in the New Testament of evil spirits being sent for punishment of believers, 1 Corinthians 5:5 and 1 Timothy 1:20. The best thing for every believer to do is to be vigilant to be continually suited in the armor of light. Every believer needs to be vigilant in their walk with God to be sure they are not in a condition where God decides to send punishment in the form of an evil spirit to inflict torment.

It is obvious from the book of Job that God permits Satan to bring attacks against believers for reasons other than punishment. Sometimes God permits the enemy to attack to benefit believers, as Paul tells about his own personal experience.

> Because of the surpassing greatness of the revelations, for this reason, to keep me from exalting myself, there was given me a thorn in the flesh, a messenger of Satan to torment me—to keep me from exalting myself! Concerning this I implored the Lord three times that it might leave me. And He has said to me, "My grace is sufficient for you, for power is perfected in weakness." Most gladly, therefore, I will rather boast about my weaknesses, so that the power of Christ may dwell in me. Therefore I am well content with weaknesses, with insults, with distresses, with persecutions, with difficulties, for Christ's sake; for when I am weak, then I am strong.
>
> 2 Corinthians 12:7–9 (NASB)

Spiritual warfare is much more than exercising authority and power over the unseen evil enemy. There will be times when this will be ineffective according to God's directives. Engaging in spiritual warfare includes the believer enduring by faith the attacks which God allows the enemy to carry out. The devil gladly takes advantage of every opportunity to afflict believers.

The goal of the evil one is to cause believers to abandon God and even to curse God as is revealed in Job 1–2. Every time a believer endures the attacks of the enemy by faith it is a testimony in the courtroom of the third heaven against Satan, who is guilty of rejecting and cursing the Creator who entrusted him with nothing but the best. Lucifer experienced nothing unpleasant that would have caused him to abandon the love relationship he had with God. Satan's fall was solely the result of his own pride and arrogance, Ezekiel 28:14–18. When believers suffer, there is temptation to reject God. The devil wants believers to follow his lead in rebelling against the Creator. Suffering believers have a reason to want to curse God. When believers endure through their suffering by faith to stand firm in their relationship with God, they are engaging in spiritual warfare that is the most damaging and effective against the enemy. It is evidence that Lucifer, who received from God only that which was good, had no cause or excuse for his rebellion and he should have humbled himself in repentance before the Creator. Although the season of suffering is very unpleasant, it is a privilege granted to faithful believers to be a living testimony in the ongoing trial of Satan and the fallen angelic realm.

> In no way alarmed by *your* opponents—which is a sign of destruction for them, but of salvation for you, and that *too*, from God. For to you it has been granted for Christ's sake, not only to believe in Him, but also to suffer for His sake,
>
> Philippians 1:28–29 (NASB)

In the midst of suffering, it is most difficult of believers to remember that the loving Father in heaven has nothing but the best in mind for them in all circumstances.

> Therefore we do not lose heart, but though our outer man is decaying, yet our inner man is being renewed day

by day. For momentary, light affliction is producing for us an eternal weight of glory far beyond all comparison, while we look not at the things which are seen, but at the things which are not seen; for the things which are seen are temporal, but the things which are not seen are eternal.

2 Corinthians 4:16–18 (NASB)

This perspective is crucial to endure the afflictions that come with standing in the armor of light to engage in the spiritual warfare. Even when a believer appears to the world to be struck down and defeated, that can be the time of greatest victory. When believers stand firm in their faith, they will be bold and secure no matter the circumstances.

Psalm 91 is about the security of the faithful believer in the midst of the spiritual war. This psalm can be edifying for those who are engaged in a conventional war against flesh and blood. However, this psalm can be most uplifting and encouraging to believers who obey the command to put on the armor of light to encounter the rulers, the powers, the world forces of this darkness, the spiritual forces of wickedness in the heavenly places.

¹He who dwells in the shelter of the Most High Will abide in the shadow of the Almighty.

²I will say to the LORD, "My refuge and my fortress, my God, in whom I trust!"

³For it is He who delivers you from the snare of the trapper and from the deadly pestilence.

⁴He will cover you with His pinions, and under His wings you may seek refuge; His faithfulness is a shield and bulwark.

⁵You will not be afraid of the terror by night, or of the arrow that flies by day;

⁶Of the pestilence that stalks in darkness, or of the destruction that lays waste at noon.

⁷A thousand may fall at your side And ten thousand at your right hand, But it shall not approach you.

⁸You will only look on with your eyes and see the recompense of the wicked.

⁹For you have made the Lord, my refuge, even the Most High, your dwelling place.

¹⁰No evil will befall you, nor will any plague come near your tent.

¹¹For He will give His angels charge concerning you, to guard you in all your ways.

¹²They will bear you up in their hands, that you do not strike your foot against a stone.

¹³You will tread upon the lion and cobra, the young lion and the serpent you will trample down.

¹⁴"Because he has loved Me, therefore I will deliver him; I will set him securely on high, because he has known My name.

¹⁵"He will call upon Me, and I will answer him; I will be with him in trouble; I will rescue him and honor him.

¹⁶"With a long life I will satisfy him and let him see My salvation."

Psalm 91 (NASB)

When believers are suited in the armor of light, not only are they wearing protective armor, but they are also protected in God's fortress, verses 1 and 2. Those who are in the fortress are protected from Satan's "deadly pestilence" and "the terror by night" and "the arrow that flies by day." These are the same arrows that Paul warns about in Ephesians 6:16. The warriors dressed in the armor of light need not fear destruction that lay waste all the world around them, verse 6. Thousands of humans, including fleshly believers, will fall prey to the enemy. The warrior who stands firm in the armor of light and does not fear will share in the victory and the glory of Jesus Christ. "You will only look on with your eyes and see the recompense of the wicked," verse 8. Those who make the Lord their refuge in the spiritual war will dwell securely in their homes, verses 9 and 10. The holy angels of God are empowered in their fight against the enemy in the unseen realm to protect the faithful warrior standing firm in faith, verses 11 and 12. It is interesting that Satan quoted these two verses to Jesus when tempting Him to jump from the pinnacle of the temple. Satan must have failed to understand the full intent of this psalm, that it is an exhortation to believers who obey the command to war against the powers of wickedness. The lion, cobra, young lion, and serpent in verse 13, which the faithful warrior will trample down, are the world forces of this darkness and the spiritual forces of wickedness that Paul lists in Ephesians 6:12. Verses 14 through 16 give God's promise of deliverance from the enemy and the promise of eternal reward: "I will set him securely on high, because he has known My name" (verse 14, NASB). There is not a safer or more secure place for any believer to be than standing firm against the enemy in the armor of light.

As was covered earlier in this chapter, the church is made up of peoples from all the races and has become a "chosen race" that transcends the boundaries of the nations.

> For there is no distinction between Jew and Greek; for the same Lord is Lord of all, abounding in riches for all who call upon Him.
>
> Romans 10:12 (NASB)

As covered at the beginning of this chapter, while Satan was busy working to prevent God from establishing Israel as the holy and priestly nation, God formed a new body on earth to be priests and a holy nation using people of all races from the nations that Satan boasts belong to him, Luke 4:5–6. John wrote in 1 John 5:19, "The whole world lies in the power of the evil one" (NASB). The holy nation, to which every Christian in the world belongs, is the only nation that is not under the power of the evil one. But that is not to say that believers can reject the authority of human governments.

Let every person be in subjection to the governing authorities. For there is no authority except from God, and those which exist are established by God. Therefore he who resists authority has opposed the ordinance of God; and they who have opposed will receive condemnation upon themselves.

Romans 13:1–2 (NASB)

It is a miracle of God that believers can be in subjection to human national governments, yet not be under the authority of Satan who has power over the nations. It is important that believers distinguish the physical realm from the spiritual realm. If believers oppose human governing authorities, they are struggling against flesh and blood, Ephesians 6:12. A battle focused solely in the physical realm will have no impact against the satanic power. In fact, such action usually gives Satan the advantage against believers. God has given believers a much better means to engage the enemy and to have a very positive impact on human governing officials at the same time. Since we are seated with Christ at the right hand of God in the heavenly places, we have authority through Christ over the entire fallen angelic realm including those who have power over the nations. From this place of power, believers can bind the powers of darkness and pray for human governing authorities to protect them from the evil plans of Satan.

First of all, then, I urge that entreaties and prayers, petitions and thanksgivings, be made on behalf of all men, for kings and all who are in authority, in order that we may lead a tranquil and quiet life in all godliness and dignity.

1 Timothy 2:1–2 (NASB)

When believers exercise their God-given authority over the powers of darkness, Satan is restrained in the power he wields over the human nations. The church empowered by the Holy Spirit is the restrainer, as was covered in the chapter "Gathering of the Faithful." God has changed the hearts of many governing authorities as a result of believers' prayers. The obedience of believers to governing authorities is a mighty witness. The only time believers are justified before God in disobeying human governments is when their law would cause believers to sin against God, Daniel 3 and 6, Acts 4:19–22 and 5:40–42.

It is crucial for believers to remember that it is totally by the grace of God that they are seated with Jesus Christ at the right hand of the Father. None of us have seated ourselves in the heavenly place. All the glory in these things belongs to God alone. God most definitely needs no help from any human or angel to defeat Satan and all the fallen angelic host and to establish His absolute dominion. It is our privilege that God has given us this once-in-eternity opportunity to participate in the war for dominion. God's purpose for including us is to shame Satan and the crafty and powerful rulers of wickedness by empowering beings made from the dust of the ground against them.

> But God has chosen the foolish things of the world to shame the wise, and God has chosen the weak things of the world to shame the things which are strong, and the base things of the world and the despised God has chosen, the things that are not, so that He may nullify the things that are, so that no man may boast before God.
>
> 1 Corinthians 1:27–29 (NASB)

Humans who are prideful and boastful are agents and allies of the satanic powers. When those people are shamed and nullified, the fallen angelic powers allied with them are also shamed and nullified. We must never think of ourselves as being able to engage the human and angelic enemy in our own strength. Believers need to be careful about their own spiritual status because the powers of darkness have many ways they can bring counterattacks. The extreme example in Scripture is the attack that came upon the sons of Sceva when they tried, by the energy of their own flesh, to confront a man held in demonic bondage, Acts 19:13–16. It is necessary to be vigilant, but we must not be fearful. Many believers fail to engage in the spiritual warfare because of fear. They are like the people in country of the Gerasenes who were gripped with fear after Jesus cast out legion from the man they severely tormented.

> And the people went out to see what had happened; and they came to Jesus, and found the man from whom the demons had gone out, sitting down at the feet of Jesus, clothed and in his right mind; and they became frightened. And those who had seen it reported to them how the man who was demon-possessed had been made well. And all the people of the country of the Gerasenes and the surrounding district asked Him to depart from them; for they were gripped with great fear; and He got into a boat, and returned.
>
> Luke 8:35–37 (NASB)

The people who sent Jesus away missed out on a great opportunity of blessing. If they had invited Jesus to stay with them, He would have revealed Himself to them through His teaching, and the Lord would have ministered healing to many of them and set many more free from demonic bondage. Certainly there were many more in that region who were enslaved to darkness besides the man set free from legion. Jesus will not manifest Himself nor His power in a place where He is not welcome, Mark 6:4–6. Believers must be vigilant in spiritual warfare, but the children of God must also be bold in engaging the enemy. God has enlisted us to put on the armor of light and battle the enemy. Believers who shrink in fear are sending away Jesus and His ministry of power and authority. Those believers will miss out on wonderful blessings and the opportunity to see God at work as happened to the people in the country of the Gerasenes.

An argument could be made that if the whole body of Christ is currently seated with Him positionally in the heavenly place of authority, then the whole body of Christ must also be the bride of Christ who will reign with Him on the earth in the kingdom. But the authority given to the church now is for the purpose of battling the powers of darkness. It is not authority to reign over the nations, as the bride will do in the kingdom of Christ. In the kingdom, all the powers of darkness will be cast off the earth and into the abyss. When Jesus Christ leaves His current place where He is seated at the right hand of the Father, then there will no longer be a place or need for the body of Christ to be seated there with Him. The full armor of God and the need for authority over the satanic forces is only for the here and now. In the kingdom, the armor of God will go away forever. Christians who have effectively used the armor of God are those who will be included in the bride of Christ. They will trade their armor for the clean, bright linen representing their righteous acts. Ideally, those who are victorious in battle are the ones who are best suited to wield authority as leaders. Power to rule in the kingdom will be given to Christians who faithfully utilized the power given to them in their temporal lives.

> His master said to him, "Well done, good and faithful slave; you were faithful with a few things, I will put you in charge of many things, enter into the joy of your master."
>
> Matthew 25:15 (NASB)

THE ETERNAL CITY OF GOD

Since the time of His resurrection and ascension, the Lord Jesus has also been in the process of building the eternal dwelling place for His bride in the third heaven, John 14:2–3. That dwelling place is the New Jerusalem. In the chapter "Dominion of the Faithful," examination is made of the prophecy in Psalm 45, which reveals a "queen in gold from Ophir" standing at the right hand of Jesus Christ. This scene is the Lamb and His eternal wife in the New Jerusalem. The queen is also referred to as the King's daughter. She is the daughter of God the Father. The end of Psalm 45 gives a prophetic description of the bride of the Lamb entering the New Jerusalem for the first time to take up residence.

> The King's daughter is all glorious within; Her clothing is interwoven with gold.
> She will be led to the King in embroidered work; The virgins, her companions who follow her, will be brought to You.
> They will be led forth with gladness and rejoicing; They will enter into the King's palace.
>
> Psalm 45:13–15 (NASB)

The virgins who are the companions of the King's daughter are believers who reside on the new earth who have access into the New Jerusalem, which will be explained later in this chapter. The queen's clothing interwoven with gold is representative of the eternal rewards given to the faithful who are included in the bride of Christ. The New Jerusalem is still in the third heaven at the time she enters the King's palace. As covered at the end of the chapter "Dominion of All in All" of this book, after the bride has entered then God the Father will move the New Jerusalem to the new earth to rest upon the eternal Mt Zion.

> And I saw the holy city, new Jerusalem, coming down out of heaven from God, made ready as a bride adorned for her husband.
>
> Revelation 21:2 (NASB)

> And one of the seven angels who had the seven bowls full of the seven last plagues, came and spoke with me, saying, "Come here, I shall show you the bride, the wife of the Lamb." And he carried me away in the Spirit to a great and high mountain, and showed me the holy city, Jerusalem, coming down out of heaven from God.
>
> Revelation 21:9–10 (NASB)

The presence of the wife of the Lamb in the New Jerusalem is what makes it to be as a bride adorned for her husband. It will be at this time that the marriage between the Lord Jesus and His bride will finally be consummated and the marriage supper of the Lamb will take place. The forming of the bride of Christ will continue through the thousand-year kingdom of Christ, so the bride will not be complete until the end of that period.

> "Let us rejoice and be glad and give the glory to Him, for the marriage of the Lamb has come and His bride has

made herself ready." It was given to her to clothe herself in fine linen, bright and clean; for the fine linen is the righteous acts of the saints.

Revelation 19:7–8 (NASB)

These are the faithful believers from human history whom Christ gathered off the earth before the start of the tribulation period. They prepare themselves as the bride of the Lamb, but the marriage supper will not take place at this point in time. These will be included with armies that come with Jesus Christ at His second coming.

And the armies which are in heaven, clothed in fine linen, white and clean, were following Him on white horses.

Revelation 19:14 (NASB)

These faithful believers will reign with Christ on the earth for a thousand years. This will include King David, who will rule over Israel during the thousand years, Ezekiel 34:23–24 and 37:24–25. Prophecy about righteous and holy believers accompanying Jesus Christ when He comes to establish His kingdom on the earth was first given in the Old Testament.

You will flee by the valley of My mountains.... Then the LORD, my God, will come, and all the holy ones with Him!

Zechariah 14:5 (NASB)

The holy ones are faithful believers from every age of human history who were resurrected at the gathering to Christ. Imagine the other great believers of human history who will reign with Christ for a thousand years. They will be ruling and leading the people living on the earth during the thousand years to be faithful that they too might be added to the bride of Christ. When the forming of the bride is complete at the end of the thousand-year kingdom, then the marriage supper of the Lamb will take place in the New Jerusalem at the top of the eternal Mt. Zion on the new earth. The marriage supper will be the start of an eternity of rejoicing.

> "For behold, I create new heavens and a new earth; And the former things will not be remembered or come to mind. "But be glad and rejoice forever in what I create; For behold, I create Jerusalem for rejoicing and her people for gladness. "I will also rejoice in Jerusalem and be glad in My people; And there will no longer be heard in her the voice of weeping and the sound of crying.
>
> Isaiah 65:17–19 (NASB)

The bride of the Lamb has the honor of being the eternal hostess who will welcome the peoples of the nations into the New Jerusalem.

> The Spirit and the bride say, "Come." And let the one who hears say, "Come." And let the one who is thirsty come; let the one who wishes take the water of life without cost.
>
> Revelation 22:17 (NASB)

In the chapter "Dominion of All in All," examination was made of the prophecies in Revelation about the wonders of the eternal New Jerusalem. Of all the wonders of the new creation, God will make His eternal city the most spectacular. The appearance from the outside of the Holy City will be astounding with the radiant glory of God and the Lamb beaming forth through the transparent walls in all directions. The marvels inside the New Jerusalem will be unparalleled by anything in the eternal creation. In writing about these eternal wonders, the Apostle John was directed to include an important warning he received from the Lord about eternal rewards.

Let the one who does wrong, still do wrong; and let the one who is filthy, still be filthy; and let the one who is righteous, still practice righteousness; and let the one who is holy, still keep himself holy. Behold, I am coming quickly, and My reward is with Me, to render to every man according to what he has done. I am the Alpha and the Omega, the first and the last, the beginning and the end. Blessed are those who wash their robes, that they may have the right to the tree of life, and may enter by the gates into the city. Outside are the dogs and the sorcerers and the immoral persons and the murderers and the idolaters, and everyone who loves and practices lying.

Revelation 22:11–15 (NASB)

The context of this passage is the rewards given by Jesus Christ for the deeds of believers in their temporal lives on the present earth. As presented in earlier chapters, the deeds of believers that the Lord will evaluate are those that come after salvation, not those before salvation. Those who "may enter the gates into the city" are contrasted to those who must remain outside the city. Those excluded from entering are those believers whose temporal lives after salvation were characterized as dogs, sorcerers, immoral persons, murders, idolaters, and liars. This is not describing unbelievers in the lake of fire, but instead these are believers on the new earth who have been denied the reward of entrance into the New Jerusalem and must spend eternity outside the gates of the city. Although they will no longer be practicing these sinful acts on the new earth, they will lose rewards for having practiced them in the temporal life. Entrance into the New Jerusalem is an eternal reward that must be earned through an obedient walk with God now. Children of God who walked in rebellion against God in their temporal lives after salvation will not be allowed into the New Jerusalem. Since these believers are denied the reward of entrance into the eternal city, the kings who rule over them on the new earth will bring the glory of their produce to the throne of God and the Lamb, Revelation 21:24. The key to receiving the reward of entrance into the New Jerusalem is the phrase in Revelation 22:14, "Blessed are those who wash their robes" (NASB). The washing represents believers confessing their sins and being repentant. It is clear in both the Old Testament and the New Testament that we are not able to live perfectly righteous lives as long as we reside in our temporal, earthly bodies. Since the children of God are prone to sin even after salvation, they must also be quick to confess and repent. Even though believers sin, they can still be righteous and keep themselves holy and thereby gain the reward of having access into the New Jerusalem and to the tree of life. This living righteousness is accomplished when believers continually "wash their robes." God gives His divine righteousness to every believer at the moment of salvation, which sets up the potential that believers can have experiential living righteousness every day. Having faith unto salvation is a one-time decision that results in a human being declared righteous in Christ.

> But to the one who does not work, but believes in Him who justifies the ungodly, his faith is reckoned as righteousness.
>
> Romans 4:5 (NASB)

Those who believe are eternally redeemed by the blood of Jesus Christ.

> Knowing that you were not redeemed with perishable things like silver or gold from your futile way of life inherited from your forefathers, but with precious blood, as of a lamb unblemished and spotless, the blood of Christ.
>
> 1 Peter 1:18–19 (NASB)

Being righteous through faith in Jesus Christ is eternal and cannot be lost. But living righteously after salvation in this temporal life is a moment by moment decision. The believer's confession of sins has to be a continual act. The washing of one's garment is not a one-time act, but must be done continually. The washing of our robes is not salvation but continual repentance and confession. The precious blood of Jesus Christ that gave us eternal redemption is the same blood of Jesus that continually cleanses us daily from all sin and unrighteousness when we confess and repent.

> But if we walk in the light as He Himself is in the light, we have fellowship with one another, and the blood of Jesus His Son cleanses us from all sin.
> If we confess our sins, He is faithful and righteous to forgive us our sins and to cleanse us from all unrighteousness.
>
> 1 John 1:7 and 9 (NASB)

It is in "the blood of Jesus His Son" that believers continually wash their robes in order to be cleansed. Daily cleansing by the blood of Jesus Christ is paramount. This truth is clarified in the prophecy the Apostle John gives about the saints of every nation from the great tribulation who will be continually before the throne of God in the New Jerusalem.

> And I said to him, "My lord, you know." And he said to me, "These are the ones who come out of the great tribulation, and they have washed their robes and made them white in the blood of the Lamb. For this reason, they are before the throne of God; and they serve Him day and night in His temple; and He who sits on the throne shall spread His tabernacle over them."
>
> Revelation 7:14 (NASB)

These saints do not have this amazing place of blessing for all eternity simply because they received eternal salvation in the time of the great tribulation. They have an eternal presence at the throne of God and the Lamb because, as believers, they lived righteous lives on the earth in a time that will be the most difficult to live for God. When the apostasy comes, there will be more opportunities than ever before in human history to satisfy the lusts of the flesh. The saints who will dare live repentant lives so as to walk in the light during the great tribulation will face persecution and martyrdom. But these believers will maintain their walk in righteousness in this most grievous time by washing their robes in the blood of the Lamb. As a result of their living repentant, righteous lives, these saints will be given the reward of having a permanent place at the throne of God, serving Him in the New Jerusalem. The death of Jesus on the cross removed the eternal consequences of our sins as far as our destiny in the lake of fire. But the sacrifice of Jesus did not remove the consequences of our sins with regard to the loss of eternal rewards. It is most important in this temporal life for the children of God to make sure they are continually in fellowship with God by confession so as to be walking in the light. There are serious eternal repercussions for failing to do so. Even the Apostle Paul feared being disqualified from the eternal rewards. Paul made a very determined effort to make sure that he would not be excluded, 1 Corinthians 9:25–27.

The list of characteristics of unfaithful believers in Revelation 22:15 (dogs sorcerers, immoral persons, murderers, idolaters, and liars) is very similar to the list Paul gives of the works that characterize believers who walk in the flesh.

> Now the deeds of the flesh are evident, which are: immorality, impurity, sensuality, idolatry, sorcery, enmities, strife, jealousy, outbursts of anger, disputes, dissensions,

factions, envying, drunkenness, carousing, and things like these, of which I forewarn you just as I have forewarned you that those who practice such things shall not inherit the kingdom of God.

Galatians 5:19–21 (NASB)

At the end of verse 21 Paul writes, "Those who practice such things shall not inherit the Kingdom of God" (NASB). The inheritance is not eternal salvation from the lake of fire but refers to having rewards in the kingdom. Unfaithful sons are still the sons of their father, but the wise father gives the inheritance only to his faithful sons. Believers who obey the command to walk in the Spirit so as to continually put to death the works of the flesh will be rewarded with entrance into the New Jerusalem. Those who refuse will have the blessing of being on the new earth, but no privilege of entrance into the New Jerusalem to the throne of God and the Lamb. The list of traits of disobedient believers in Revelation 22:15 closely matches the list of traits of unbelievers cast into the lake of fire.

But for the cowardly and unbelieving and abominable and murderers and immoral persons and sorcerers and idolaters and all liars, their part will be in the lake that burns with fire and brimstone, which is the second death.

Revelation 21:8 (NASB)

When believers walk in the flesh they are not distinguishable from unbelievers. The one big difference between these two lists, however, is that those who are cast into the lake of fire are the "unbelieving." They are not saved through faith.

Other passages in Revelation also reveal that entrance into the wondrous New Jerusalem and access to the tree of life are limited to those who are the faithful children of God.

> And nothing unclean and no one who practices abomi-
> nation and lying, shall ever come into it, but only those
> whose names are written in the Lamb's book of life.
>
> Revelation 21:27 (NASB)

Those who are "unclean" and the "one who practices abomination
and lying" do accurately describe the unbelievers who are cast
into the lake of fire. But to say that those who are in the eternal
lake of fire will never enter the New Jerusalem would be stating
the obvious because they won't even be on the new earth.
This characterization also accurately describes believers who
continually walk in the flesh after their salvation and actually
is another reference to the same believers who lived like "dogs"
and "immoral persons" in their temporal lives after being saved,
Revelation 22:15. This passage also states that "only those whose
names are written in the Lamb's book of life" shall have entrance
into the New Jerusalem. It will be beneficial at this point to
compare Scripture with Scripture regarding the Lamb's Book
of Life.

Every human who is a child of God by faith has had their
name written in the Lamb's Book of Life since the foundation of
the world. All humans who are unbelievers have never had their
name written in the Book of Life. In the great tribulation period,
the unbelievers will easily be deceived by the Antichrist and will
follow after him to receive his mark and worship his image.

> And those who dwell on the earth will wonder, whose
> name has not been written in the book of life from the
> foundation of the world, when they see the beast, that he
> was and is not and will come.
>
> Revelation 17:8 (NASB)

> And all who dwell on the earth will worship him, whose names have not been written in the Book of Life of the Lamb slain from the foundation of the world.
>
> Revelation 13:8 (NKJV)

God was able to write the names of His children of faith in the Lamb's Book of Life from the foundation of the world only because the Lamb was slain from the foundation of the world. In His omniscience, God the Father has known that His plan would require the sacrifice of His Son for the sins of the entire human race. In His omniscience, God has also known since before the beginning of creation all those who would accept by faith His love gift offered to the human race. These are the only ones whose names God has recorded in the Lamb's book of life. All humans who are unbelievers have never had their names written in the Lamb's Book of Life and will be thrown into the eternal lake of fire to suffer the eternal second death.

> And death and Hades were thrown into the lake of fire. This is the second death, the lake of fire. And if anyone's name was not found written in the book of life, he was thrown into the lake of fire.
>
> Revelation 20:14–15 (NASB)

There is a third category of humans who have had their names written in the Lamb's Book of Life from the foundation of the world, but who will have their names erased. Jesus Christ gives a warning to the believers at the church in Sardis that this will happen to believers who have become spiritually lethargic.

> He who overcomes shall thus be clothed in white garments; and I will not erase his name from the book of life, and I will confess his name before My Father, and before His

angels. He who has an ear, let him hear what the Spirit says to the churches.

Revelation 3:5–6 (NASB)

David also writes about the removal of peoples' names from the Book of Life in one of his prophetic Psalms about the suffering Messiah.

Reproach has broken my heart, and I am so sick. And I looked for sympathy, but there was none, and for comforters, but I found none. They also gave me gall for my food, and for my thirst they gave me vinegar to drink. May their table before them become a snare; and when they are in peace, may it become a trap. May their eyes grow dim so that they cannot see, and make their loins shake continually. Pour out Thine indignation on them, and may Thy burning anger overtake them. May their camp be desolate; may none dwell in their tents. For they have persecuted him whom Thou Thyself hast smitten, and they tell of the pain of those whom Thou hast wounded. Do Thou add iniquity to their iniquity, and may they not come into Thy righteousness. May they be blotted out of the book of life, and may they not be recorded with the righteous.

Psalm 69:20–28 (NASB)

This is prophetic of those Israelites who rejected Jesus as the promised Messiah and called for His crucifixion. Many of those Jews have had their names written in the Book of Life from the foundation of the world and they have eternal life because they believed the promises of the coming Messiah, but they rejected Jesus as the fulfillment of those prophesies. As punishment, God sent the Roman army to make their camp, Jerusalem, desolate in 70 AD. Jesus foretold this coming destruction in Matthew 23:37–38. However, in addition to this temporal destruction, the

Jews of that generation who rejected Jesus as the Messiah will have their names blotted out of the Book of Life. The action of Jesus Christ to remove the names of believers from the Book of Life will take place at His judgment. Every human, believer and unbeliever, will stand before one of the judgment seats of Jesus Christ. As covered in the chapter "Dominion of the Faithful," there are three different appearings of Jesus Christ given in the prophecies in which humans are resurrected and come face-to-face with their Creator. His first appearing for resurrection is to gather the faithful, 1 Thessalonians 4 and 1 Corinthians 15. His second appearing for resurrection is at His second coming, Revelation 20:4–6. His third appearing for resurrection is when He is seated on the great white throne, Revelation 20:11–15. Those who are resurrected at each of these occasions will be judged regarding their eternal destinies and rewards. The judicial procedures and evaluation process at each of these judgments are given in numerous Scriptures.

> Many of those who sleep in the dust of the ground will awake, these to everlasting life, but the others to disgrace and everlasting contempt.
>
> Those who have insight will shine brightly like the brightness of the expanse of heaven, and those who lead the many to righteousness, like the stars forever and ever.
>
> Daniel 12:2–3 (NASB)

> For no man can lay a foundation other than the one which is laid, which is Jesus Christ. Now if any man builds upon the foundation with gold, silver, precious stones, wood, hay, straw, each man's work will become evident; for the day will show it, because it is to be revealed with fire; and the fire itself will test the quality of each man's work.
>
> If any man's work which he has built upon it remains, he shall receive a reward.

If any man's work is burned up, he shall suffer loss; but he himself shall be saved, yet so as through fire.

1 Corinthians 3:12–15 (NASB)

Then I saw a great white throne and Him who sat upon it, from whose presence earth and heaven fled away, and no place was found for them.

And I saw the dead, the great and the small, standing before the throne, and books were opened; and another book was opened, which is the book of life; and the dead were judged from the things which were written in the books, according to their deeds.

And the sea gave up the dead which were in it, and death and Hades gave up the dead which were in them; and they were judged, every one *of* them according to their deeds.

Then death and Hades were thrown into the lake of fire. This is the second death, the lake of fire.

And if anyone's name was not found written in the book of life, he was thrown into the lake of fire.

Revelation 20:11–15 (NASB)

Daniel 12:2–3 includes prophecy of the resurrection and judgment of believers and unbelievers. At the time Daniel wrote this it was not revealed that there are actually three resurrections. However, all three of these passages have commonality in that they define the evaluation of works and the resulting consequences. In 1 Corinthians 3:12–15, Paul gives prophecy that applies to the judgment for believers only. This is the evaluation process for the faithful and the unfaithful believers from human history. Faithful believers are gathered to Christ before the start of the tribulation period as Paul reveals in 1 Thessalonians 4:13-18 and 1 Corinthians 15:51-58. Since only faithful believers are resurrected at this gathering, none of these believers will have all their works burned and they will receive rewards. Additionally, this describes the evaluation process of the martyrs who will be resurrected as described in Revelation 20:4–6 at the start of the thousand-year kingdom of Christ. Again, only faithful believers will be resurrected at that time. The last and final resurrection and judgment seat will be the great white throne prophesied in Revelation 20:11–15. This final resurrection will include all of the people who died during the thousand-year kingdom of Christ, the unfaithful believers from all of human history, and unbelievers from all of human history. As each person comes before the judgment seat of Jesus Christ, a search will first be made in the Book of Life to determine if their name has been recorded since the foundation of the world. If a person's name is found then that person will in no way experience the lake of fire and is guaranteed to be included in the eternal estate. Then, as described in 1 Corinthians 3:12–15, Jesus Christ makes further evaluation of the person's temporal life as a believer. Some of those resurrected will be faithful believers from the time of the thousand-year kingdom of Christ. Every believer who has been faithful to the Lord in his or her temporal life after salvation will receive eternal rewards, including access to the New Jerusalem. But if the Judge determines that a believer walked in continual sin and disobedience, having no regard for serving Him after salvation, eternal rewards will be denied and Jesus will erase that believer's name from the Book of Life. This does not mean that the individual is then going to the lake of fire. That issue was resolved when the person first came before the judgment seat and their name was found in the Book of Life. The erasing of the believer's name is like the removal of a person's name from a will so they receive no inheritance. The believers whose names are erased will lose the inheritance of eternal rewards. Because their name is no longer in the Book of Life, they are eternally denied the awesome reward and joy of having entrance into the New Jerusalem and access to the throne of God and the Lamb and to the tree of life. They will be on the new earth, but they will forever have to stay outside the gates of the New Jerusalem, Revelation 22:15.

The prophet and King David also wrote prophecy that gives insight about who will have the great honor of being in the presence of the throne of God and who will be denied this amazing experience.

> Lord, who may abide in Thy tent? Who may dwell on Thy holy hill? He who walks with integrity, and works righteousness, and speaks truth in his heart. He does not slander with his tongue, nor does evil to his neighbor, nor takes up a reproach against his friend; In whose eyes a reprobate is despised, but who honors those who fear the Lord; He swears to his own hurt, and does not change; He does not put out his money at interest, Nor does he take a bribe against the innocent. He who does these things will never be shaken.
>
> Psalm 15 (NASB)

> My eyes shall be upon the faithful of the land, that they may dwell with me; He who walks in a blameless way is the one who will minister to me. He who practices deceit shall not dwell within my house; He who speaks falsehood shall not maintain his position before me.
>
> Psalm 101:6–7 (NASB)

There will be no tents of wickedness on the new earth, but there will be the dwellings of those whose names were erased from the Lamb's Book of Life because they lived in wickedness in their temporal lives after salvation. These are the dogs and the sorcerers and the immoral persons outside the gates, Revelation 22: 15. Psalm 84 will have whole new relevance when sung before the throne of God and the Lamb in the New Jerusalem.

For a day in Thy courts is better than a thousand outside. I would rather stand at the threshold of the house of my God, than dwell in the tents of wickedness. For the Lord God is a sun and shield; the Lord gives grace and glory; no good thing does He withhold from those who walk uprightly. O Lord of hosts, how blessed is the man who trusts in Thee!

Psalm 84:10–12 (NASB)

Life on the new earth will be many times better than life in this present world, but one day in the New Jerusalem will be better than a thousand days anywhere else in the new creation. In other words, the experience of the New Jerusalem will be indescribable. No words will be adequate to communicate the wonder of it all. There is an eternity of thousands of days coming. For all eternity people are not going to be able to get enough of being in the presence of God. Only believers who walk in obedience in their temporal life after salvation will have access to the eternal Mt. Zion and entrance into the New Jerusalem.

In the letters from Jesus Christ to the seven churches, each letter ends with promises to "he who overcomes," Revelation 2–3. The promises made to the overcomers are all eternal rewards related to sharing in the dominion of Jesus Christ. The Greek word translated "overcome" also means "conquer or prevail." Some believe that overcoming is in reference to receiving eternal salvation. The belief is based on 1 John 5:5. But the use of this word implies the fighting of a battle. Eternal salvation is given as a gift. The battles to be fought come after salvation. The apostle John, who wrote Revelation, uses this same word numerous times in his 1 John epistle. Every use in 1 John is in the context of the believer's battle against the world, the flesh and the devil after salvation.

> I have written to you, young men, because you are strong, and the word of God abides in you, and you have overcome the evil one.
>
> 1 John 2:14 (NASB)

In this passage John is writing about the believer's battle to "overcome the evil one." The strength needed for this battle of faith comes only by having the Word of God abiding in us.

> and every spirit that does not confess Jesus is not from God; and this is the spirit of the antichrist, of which you have heard that it is coming, and now it is already in the world. You are from God, little children, and have overcome them; because greater is He who is in you than he who is in the world.
>
> 1 John 4:4 (NASB)

Here John uses the word *overcome* in relation to the Holy Spirit given to indwell every believer at the point of salvation. The empowerment given by the Holy Spirit is crucial to every believer in overcoming the spiritual enemies of this temporal life, including discernment of the lies of the Antichrist, which continue to deceive the world. In 1 John, the apostle is contrasting the believer who walks as the new self in the power of the Holy Spirit with the believer who continually walks in the flesh. The new self is born of the Spirit and the old self is born of the flesh at physical birth.

> That which is born of the flesh is flesh, and that which is born of the Spirit is spirit. Do not marvel that I said to you, "You must be born again."
>
> John 3:6–7 (NASB)

The new-self born of the Spirit cannot sin but will always keep the commandments of God. In contrast, the old-flesh self can do nothing but sin. Keeping God's commandments is not burdensome to the new self because the Spirit enables obedience. The new self, born at salvation, is of God and knows God. The old self is not of God and does not know God.

> Whoever believes that Jesus is the Christ is born of God, and everyone who loves Him who begot also loves him who is begotten of Him.
>
> 1 John 5:1 (NKJV)

> For whatever is born of God overcomes the world. And this is the victory that has overcome the world—our faith. Who is he who overcomes the world, but he who believes that Jesus is the Son of God?
>
> 1 John 5:4–5 (NKJV)

> And this is the testimony: that God has given us eternal life, and this life is in His Son. He who has the Son has life; he who does not have the Son of God does not have life. These things I have written to you who believe in the name of the Son of God, that you may know that you have eternal life, and that you may continue to believe in the name of the Son of God.
>
> 1 John 5:11–13 (NKJV)

In verse 1, John assures us that anyone who believes Jesus is the Christ is born as a child of God. This fact is based on the work of Jesus Christ and cannot be reversed. Nobody can undo a spiritual birth any more than a physical birth. In verses 11 and 12, John assures us that anyone who has the Son of God has life, meaning eternal life. In verse 13, to make sure we understand, John explains clearly that his purpose for writing these things is so we who believe in the Son "may know that you have eternal life." This last phrase in verse 13, "and that you may continue to believe in the name of the Son of God," is important because it explains verses 4 and 5. In verses 4 and 5, John again uses the word "overcome" when writing about our battle against the world after salvation. Our faith that overcomes the world is our moment-by-moment living faith and not our salvation faith. That continuing faith is the faith that overcomes the world. That living faith after salvation is the basis for our eternal rewards. A continual focus on the Son of God by faith is crucial to our overcoming. Those who fail to continue believing in the Son after salvation will begin to doubt their salvation, of which John is trying to assure us in his writing. In order to overcome the world, each of us must first overcome our old-flesh self. Children who fail to continue focusing by faith on the Son of God will not overcome the world, they will not know the Son through personal fellowship, and they will not keep his commandments; and they are liars if they say they do.

> The one who says, "I have come to know Him," and does not keep His commandments, is a liar, and the truth is not in him.
>
> 1 John 2:4 (NASB)

Without the persistent daily focus of faith on the Son through the Word of God, we will live in the sin of our old-flesh self, depriving the Son of God of the fellowship He craves to have with us. Believers who deny the Son that fellowship in their temporal lives after salvation will be denied eternal rewards by the Son.

Based on John's other writings, his use of the word *overcome* is not referring to salvation by faith but is related to the believer's temporal life battle of faith after salvation. In Revelation 2 and 3, five of the seven letters from Jesus warn the churches that their activities will result in both temporal punishment and the loss of eternal rewards. The promises of rewards at the end of each of the letters to the seven churches will be given only to believers who overcome. Every believer throughout the history of the church, and all human history, has had the potential of receiving these rewards if their lives have been characterized by overcoming the world, the flesh, and the devil.

> To him who overcomes, I will grant to eat of the tree of life, which is in the Paradise of God.
>
> Revelation 2:7 (NASB)

The tree of life will be only in the New Jerusalem where those who have been faithful will be allowed to enter.

> I am coming quickly; hold fast what you have, in order that no one take your crown. He who overcomes, I will make him a pillar in the temple of My God, and he will not go out from it anymore; and I will write upon him the name of My God, and the name of the city of My God, the new Jerusalem, which comes down out of heaven from My God, and My new name.
>
> Revelation 3:11–12 (NASB)

Here is a promise to the ones who overcome that they will have the eternal reward of a permanent place in the New Jerusalem, not ever having to go out from the glorious eternal temple of God. This is given only to the faithful believer who overcomes so as to become the bride of Christ. Only believers who make up the bride of Christ will have permanent residence in the New Jerusalem.

> And to the angel of the church in Smyrna write: The first and the last, who was dead, and has come to life, says this:

"I know your tribulation and your poverty (but you are rich), and the blasphemy by those who say they are Jews and are not, but are a synagogue of Satan. Do not fear what you are about to suffer. Behold, the devil is about to cast some of you into prison, that you may be tested, and you will have tribulation ten days. Be faithful until death, and I will give you the crown of life. He who has an ear, let him hear what the Spirit says to the churches. He who overcomes shall not be hurt by the second death."

Revelation 2:8–11 (NASB)

This is one of the two churches to which Jesus gave no rebuke. The Smyrna church had no areas of disobedience that were jeopardizing their receiving of eternal rewards. Jesus tells them they are rich, referring to the eternal wealth they had already built up for themselves which they will receive at His judgment seat. This church was facing physical death and needed the encouragement of the eternal life waiting for them. Jesus starts the letter by reminding them that He had been dead but had come back to life. They are promised "the crown of life" if they are faithful until death. Jesus then tells them and us that those who overcome will not be hurt by the second death. In the Greek, John uses a double negative to add emphasis that "by no means" or "in no way" will the one who overcomes be hurt by the second death. The Greek word translated *hurt* can also mean "to act unjustly, to injure, to wrong, to treat unjustly." So a more literal translation would be this: "The overcoming one shall in no way be unjustly injured by the second death." The second death is the lake of fire.

And death and Hades were thrown into the lake of fire. This is the second death, the lake of fire. And if anyone's name was not found written in the book of life, he was thrown into the lake of fire.

Revelation 20:14–15 (NASB)

In the letter to the church at Smyrna, Jesus Christ could be telling us that the believer who fails to overcome in their temporal life after salvation will be justly thrown into the lake of fire. But Jesus does not use the harsh words *thrown into* as is used regarding those whose names were never written in the Book of Life. In the letter to the Smyrna church, Jesus uses the word *hurt*, which implies a lesser degree of punishment that is related to the second death. The hurt is associated with believers being denied access to the New Jerusalem so that they miss out on a very marvelous aspect of the eternal life. The work of Jesus on the cross procures and secures the basic eternal life for everyone who will receive the gift by faith. The works of the believer after salvation procure and secure an abundant life.

> The thief comes only to steal, and kill, and destroy; I came that they might have life, and might have it abundantly. I am the good shepherd; the good shepherd lays down His life for the sheep.
>
> John 10:10–11 (NASB)

Jesus came that all who believe that He died and rose again from the dead will possess eternal life as a gift. But the Good Shepherd desires that we all advance beyond having basic eternal life to gaining abundant eternal life. Eternal life is given as a gift, and it cannot be lost. The abundant life is given as a reward of inheritance that must be earned. The reward of abundant life is lost or gained depending on each believer's obedience and faithfulness. All who have the gift of eternal life will have, at a minimum, life on the new earth. Life on the new earth is going to be wonderful, but the abundant life exists in the New Jerusalem. Believers who are excluded will not possess the abundant eternal life. They won't possess the same eternal life that faithful believers who overcome will possess. They are eternally dead with regard to the abundant life. Unfaithful believers are eternally and justly hurt or injured by a form of second death. These are the same disobedient believers who will have their names erased from the Book of Life when they are judged at the great white throne. Like the unbelievers in the eternal lake of fire, they too will be eternally separated from the presence of God, but without the eternally agony of burning in the fire and brimstone. So those disobedient believers are, in a way, suffering a form of the second death. Existence in the eternal lake of fire is the ultimate second death. Existence in the New Jerusalem is the ultimate eternal life. Believers on the new earth who are excluded from entrance into the New Jerusalem will have eternal life and will certainly be better off than the unbelievers in the lake of fire. However, they will also be eternally denied the most desirable and wonderful experience of standing before the throne of God and the Lamb and many other blessings that go along with that honor. The unfaithful who are denied access into the New Jerusalem will obviously not occupy any of the dwelling places that Jesus is preparing for His bride in the Father's house.

> In My Father's house are many dwelling places; if it were not so, I would have told you; for I go to prepare a place for you. And if I go and prepare a place for you, I will come again, and receive you to Myself; that where I am, there you may be also.
>
> John 14:2–3 (NASB)

Jesus communicated this prophetic promise to eleven men, all who were faithful to His calling. As revealed in the chapter "Gathering of the Faithful," Jesus will not receive unfaithful believers to Himself when He comes to take His eternal bride off the earth. The unfaithful will have their dwelling places on the new earth. But the faithful overcomers that Jesus returns to receive to Himself will enjoy the dwelling places He is preparing for them in the New Jerusalem. Jesus revealed His loving purpose and desire for doing this, "that where I am, there you may be also." This means an eternal physical presence with Jesus Christ. When Jesus returns to gather the faithful believers of human history, they will be with Him where He is for all eternity.

> Then we who are alive and remain shall be caught up together with them in the clouds to meet the Lord in the air, and thus we shall always be with the Lord.
>
> 1 Thessalonians 4:17 (NASB)

Only those who have dwelling places in the New Jerusalem will "always be with the Lord." Therefore, only those who have an eternal presence with the Lord will be gathered off the earth by the Lord. Jesus is personally and lovingly preparing a special place for each faithful believer who will have the reward of eternal presence with Him in the New Jerusalem. Everyone who has residence in or access to the New Jerusalem will definitely have cause for rejoicing, and Jesus Christ will rejoice with them.

> For behold, I create new heavens and a new earth; And the former things shall not be remembered or come to mind. But be glad and rejoice forever in what I create; For behold, I create Jerusalem for rejoicing, And her people for gladness. I will also rejoice in Jerusalem, and be glad in My people; And there will no longer be heard in her the voice of weeping and the sound of crying.
>
> Isaiah 65:17–19 (NASB)

The thought of being excluded from the rejoicing in the New Jerusalem should motivate every believer to be diligent to walk in a manner worthy of their salvation. Imagine what a glorious experience it will be to see Jesus Christ in the New Jerusalem rejoicing and to hear the eternal King expressing His gladness in His people.

In the chapter "Dominion of All in All" of this book, examination was made of prophecies in Isaiah 30:6 and Revelation 21:22–23 about the radiance of the Father and the Son in the New Jerusalem. Isaiah wrote that the radiance of God will be seven times brighter than the sun. It would be impossible for humans to approach such radiance in the earthly bodies that we occupy in this temporal life. The eternal resurrection body that God will give to each of us will be capable of being in the presence of such radiant glory. Being in the physical presence of such glory will be the ultimate experience. We will each crave that presence with all our being—body, soul, heart, spirit, and mind. The experience will be immensely fulfilling physically, emotionally, and mentally beyond anything we can imagine. This fellowship in the presence of God is the very purpose for which the Lord created us. Those who are excluded from the New Jerusalem and the physical presence of God will have resurrection bodies capable of being present in the radiant glory of God. They will have the hunger physically, mentally, and emotionally for this fulfillment. Their physical bodies will yearn for the warmth of His radiance that is seven times more intense than the sun. They will be like those who seek to get warm, but they are cut off from the place of heat physically, emotionally, and mentally. In their temporal lives after salvation, they yearned to feed the lust of their flesh and had no yearning to draw close to God in a personal relationship. Since being close to God had not been important to them, they will be denied the experience of standing in His glorious presence in the New Jerusalem. Those who seek to draw near to God in this temporal life find their hunger for God continually grows. The more a believer experiences God, the more the hunger for Him intensifies. Those who have grown to the extent that they crave God's appearing will be rewarded by having their yearning eternally fulfilled. This is the abundant life humans were designed to experience. This is the Creator's purpose for humans and angels. Believers who refuse God's purpose in this temporal life will have the yearning for God in the eternal life to come, but that yearning will remain unfulfilled because their names have been erased from the Lamb's Book of Life. They are justly hurt by being dead to the abundant life.

When two people grow close to each other, they become so occupied with each other that they just naturally tell other people about their experiences together. The same is true for believers who draw close to God in a personal relationship in this temporal life. Looking again at Jesus's letter to the church at Sardis, another reward that Jesus promises to those who overcome is that He will confess their names before the Father.

> He who overcomes shall thus be clothed in white garments; and I will not erase his name from the book of life, and I will confess his name before My Father, and before His angels.
>
> Revelation 3:5 (NASB)

This correlates with the teaching Jesus gave to His disciples warning them about the cost of being His witness in the world.

> Everyone therefore who shall confess Me before men, I will also confess him before My Father who is in heaven. But whoever shall deny Me before men, I will also deny him before My Father who is in heaven.
>
> Matthew 10:32–33 (NASB)

In the context of this verse, Jesus is warning his disciples about dealing with intimidation and persecution from those who want to stop the witness of Jesus. Believers who make no effort to draw close to God in the temporal life will be fearful and have no desire to tell anyone else about the Savior. In fact, they will be embarrassed to openly mention the precious name of Jesus Christ to others. Their very lives deny they even know Jesus Christ, even though they have been saved by His grace. Not only will these unfaithful believers be denied access into the New Jerusalem and the throne of God and the Lamb, but Jesus will also deny them before the Father just as they had denied Jesus in their temporal lives after salvation. Jesus will be embarrassed to mention them just as they had been embarrassed to draw near to Jesus Christ and to own a personal relationship with Him in this dark world. During the time of Jesus, many of the rulers of Israel believed the testimony of Jesus, but they refused to confess Him publicly because they feared the Pharisees and loved the approval of men more than the approval of God, John 12:42–43. When Jesus confesses believers' names before the Father, He is giving approval and accolades to those believers. The rulers of Israel craved the approval of men instead, so they followed after the Pharisees in a self-righteous ascetic lifestyle. Self-righteousness will not result in a close intimate relationship with God any more than an immoral, licentious lifestyle will. Both lifestyles are works of the flesh, both lifestyles deny God the personal relationship He desires, both lifestyles result in believers having their names denied by Jesus before the Father, and both lifestyles result in believers being eternally excluded from the New Jerusalem and access to the throne of God and the Lamb. Only believers who draw close to God through faith, in the renewing of their minds by the power of the Holy Spirit and God's eternal Word, will overcome the fleshly pitfalls of immorality and self-righteousness. Only believers renewed in their minds over time will personally know Jesus Christ so as to have uninhibited public expression of their love for Him by their words and their deeds. Jesus will gladly reward such believers by confessing their names before the Father. In the chapter "Dominion of All in All," examination was made of prophecies about the eternal promised land that Israel will occupy around the eternal Holy Mountain of God. They will have the most desirable location on the new earth. But there will be Israelites who will be denied access to the New Jerusalem. Many Israelites, like the rulers at the time of Jesus, believed the promises of God about the Messiah, but rejected Jesus as the fulfillment of that promise. As covered earlier in this chapter, Psalm 69:20-28 is prophecy that their names will be blotted out from the Book of Life. The regret of these Israelites will probably be the greatest of all, being in such close proximity to the New Jerusalem, but unable to enter into the radiance of God's glory.

Our lives after salvation is the only opportunity we have for all eternity to prove ourselves worthy to share in the dominion of Christ. Christians who take up the challenge will have unfathomable privileges and rewards in the life to come. It is crucial that believers not live for the here and now, but rather for the age to come.

> If then you have been raised up with Christ, keep seeking the things above, where Christ is, seated at the right hand of God. Set your mind on the things above, not on the things that are on earth. For you have died and your life is hidden with Christ in God. When Christ, who is our life, is revealed, then you also will be revealed with Him in glory.
>
> Colossians 3:1–4 (NASB)

The bride will be revealed with Jesus Christ in glory as she follows Him on white horses from heaven to the earth. This prophetic promise is conditional on: "Set your mind on things above... then you also will be revealed with Him in glory" Colossians 3:2 and 4 (NASB). There are many evidences in the eternal Word that being included in the gathering of faithful believers by Jesus Christ and having access to the New Jerusalem are conditional upon obedience. Therefore these are truths that every believer should be motivated to heed because the stakes are high. Jesus revealed that there are many dwelling places in the Father's house, the New Jerusalem. The Apostle John tells us how big the New Jerusalem will be.

> And the city is laid out as a square, and its length is as great as the width; and he measured the city with the rod, fifteen hundred miles; its length and width and height are equal.
>
> Revelation 21:16 (NASB)

Certainly there will be room for many dwelling places as Jesus promised. But John also reveals that there will be a lot of dwelling area on the new earth because there will be no sea.

> And I saw a new heaven and a new earth; for the first heaven and the first earth passed away, and there is no longer any sea.
>
> Revelation 21:1 (NASB)

Currently two-thirds of the earth is covered with water. The new earth will have three times more usable dwelling area than the current earth. Eternal children of God from all ages of human history will occupy the new earth and the New Jerusalem. Some will have a permanent place at the throne of God day and night, Revelation 7:15. Those who are the bride of Christ are the only ones who will have permanent residence in the many dwelling places that Jesus has prepared for His bride in the New Jerusalem, John 14:2–3. Many more will have residence on the new earth, since there is much more living area on the new earth than in the New Jerusalem. Of those who live on the new earth, many will have access into the New Jerusalem and the throne of God. These are the virgins who are the companions of the King's daughter, Psalm 45.

Kings' daughters are among Your noble ladies; At Your right hand stands the queen in gold from Ophir.

Psalm 45:9 (NASB)

The King's daughter is all glorious within; Her clothing is interwoven with gold.

She will be led to the King in embroidered work; The virgins, her companions who follow her, Will be brought to You.

Psalm 45:13–14 (NASB)

The "Kings' daughters" (plural) in verse 9 and the "virgins" in verse 14 are designations for the people who live on the earth and have access into the New Jerusalem. These are also those who are rulers over the nations on the new earth. The "King's daughter" (singular) and the "Queen in gold from Ophir" are other titles for the bride of Christ, who has permanent residence in the New Jerusalem and will not go out from it anymore, Revelation 3:12. The virgins who are companions of the bride are believers who have purified themselves in the temporal life, but not to the level of devotion that believers who are the bride of Christ achieved. Believers who are the virgins will be resurrected and gathered off the earth to Christ at the same time the Christ gathers His bride. The bride and her companions will be gathered at the same time.

There will also be others who live on the new earth who will be denied entrance through the gates of the New Jerusalem because their names have been erased from the Lamb's Book of Life. The Apostle John provides seemingly unimportant information about the New Jerusalem that needs to be given serious consideration. For one thing, the gates will never be closed, Revelation 21:25. But each gate will also have an attendant.

> It had a great and high wall, with twelve gates, and at the gates twelve angels; and names were written on them, which are those of the twelve tribes of the sons of Israel.
>
> Revelation 21:12 (NASB)

Maybe the angels are there only as greeters. Or, maybe they are there with the Lamb's Book of Life checking names and denying access to those whose names have been erased.

> And he measured its wall, seventy-two yards, according to human measurements, which are also angelic measurements. And the material of the wall was jasper; and the city was pure gold, like clear glass. The foundation stones of the city wall were adorned with every kind of precious stone.
>
> Revelation 21:17–19 (NASB)

Maybe the "great and high wall" around the city is just for appearance, as it will be beautifully adorned. Or, maybe the beautiful wall is to restrict access into the New Jerusalem. If everyone had unlimited access into the New Jerusalem, there would be no need for a wall around the eternal city of God with twelve gates spaced five hundred miles apart, if they are spaced evenly around the high wall. This is interesting to consider in light of a prophetic parable from Jesus that is recorded, Luke 13:24-30.

Believers have known about and conducted their lives in anticipation of the New Jerusalem for thousands of years. In the account of the life of Abraham in the book of Genesis, no mention is made that God had given him any information about the New Jerusalem. In Genesis 13:14–15, God promised Abraham that his descendants would have eternal possession of the promised land. The writer of Hebrews, however, reveals additional promises and prophecies were given to Abraham about the New Jerusalem that motivated him to live in the obedience of faith.

> By faith Abraham, when he was called, obeyed by going out to a place which he was to receive for an inheritance; and he went out, not knowing where he was going. By faith he lived as an alien in the land of promise, as in a foreign land, dwelling in tents with Isaac and Jacob, fellow heirs of the same promise; for he was looking for the city which has foundations, whose architect and builder is God.
>
> Hebrews 11:8–10 (NASB)

> All these died in faith, without receiving the promises, but having seen them and having welcomed them from a distance, and having confessed that they were strangers and exiles on the earth. But as it is, they desire a better country, that is a heavenly one. Therefore God is not ashamed to be called their God; for He has prepared a city for them. By faith Abraham, when he was tested, offered up Isaac; and he who had received the promises was offering up his only begotten son; it was he to whom it was said, "In Isaac your descendants shall be called." He considered that God is able to raise men even from the dead; from which he also received him back as a type.
>
> Hebrew 11:16–19 (NASB)

Abraham's faith in the promise of eternal life in the eternal city of God enabled him to be obedient in offering his son of promise as a sacrifice to the Lord. If the promise of the eternal city was so motivating to Abraham, Isaac, and Jacob, then that promise should certainly be motivating to believers of this age to walk in the obedience of faith. The writer of Hebrews exhorts believers to make whatever sacrifices are necessary in following Jesus Christ in order to gain the eternal city of God.

> Therefore Jesus also, that He might sanctify the people through His own blood, suffered outside the gate. So, let us go out to Him outside the camp, bearing His reproach. For here we do not have a lasting city, but we are seeking the city which is to come.
>
> Hebrews 13:12–14 (NASB)

All the faithful believers listed in Hebrews 11 are those who will be included in the bride of Christ, the eternal royal priesthood, the holy nation, and will have eternal dwelling places in the New Jerusalem. There will be many nations on the new earth, Revelation 21:24, but the residents of the New Jerusalem will be the eternal holy nation made up of faithful believers from every period of human history. As with Abraham, all these faithful believers "desired a better country, that is a heavenly one." They lived their lives "so that they might obtain a better resurrection" (Hebrews 11:35, NASB). For the faithful believers identified in Hebrew 11, the better resurrection will be when Jesus returns to gather His bride off the earth before the time of the tribulation. The list starts with Abel from early in human history, Hebrews 11:4. The writer of Hebrews indicates this is only a partial list of faithful believers.

> And what more shall I say? For time will fail me if I tell of Gideon, Barak, Samson, Jephthah, of David and Samuel and the prophets,
>
> Hebrew 11:32 (NASB)

The future new heaven and new earth are going to be beyond anything we can imagine at this present time. God has subjected this present world to groaning with earthquakes, volcanoes, tsunamis, unstable weather, and natural disasters to cause the human race to understand the effect Adam's sin has had on the creation, Romans 8:19–22. Even so, the current earth is filled with much natural beauty and many created wonders from the hand of God. Certainly the new earth will be all the more filled with beauty and awesome marvels of God's creative genius. It will be a blessed, eternally stable place to live with no more sin or fallen nature. But life on the new earth will be more blessed for some than for others. Jesus gave prophecy about life in the eternal future when the Roman centurion came to Him, imploring Jesus to heal his servant.

> And when Jesus entered Capernaum, a centurion came to Him, imploring Him, and saying, "Lord, my servant is lying paralyzed at home, fearfully tormented." Jesus said to him, "I will come and heal him." But the centurion said, "Lord, I am not worthy for You to come under my roof, but just say the word, and my servant will be healed. For I also am a man under authority, with soldiers under me; and I say to this one, 'Go!' and he goes, and to another, 'Come!' and he comes, and to my slave, 'Do this!' and he does it." Now when Jesus heard this, He marveled and said to those who were following, "Truly I say to you, I have not found such great faith with anyone in Israel. I say to you that many will come from east and west, and recline at the table with Abraham, Isaac and Jacob in the kingdom of heaven; but the sons of the kingdom will be cast out into the outer darkness; in that place there will be weeping and gnashing of teeth." And Jesus said to the centurion, "Go; it shall be done for you as you have believed." And the servant was healed that very moment.
>
> Matthew 8:11–13 (NASB)

In responding to the centurion, Jesus took opportunity to give a prophecy about life in the "kingdom of heaven," which is the eternal kingdom on the new earth. Being in the "outer darkness" is an eternal status. The "sons of the kingdom" refers to Jews. The Jews are God's chosen people to whom He has specifically made prophetic promises of the eternal kingdom, which the Jews at the time of Jesus forfeited because of their rejection of the Messiah. Jesus came proclaiming the good news of the promised kingdom and showed many miracles to validate His claim, Matthew 4:23. But most of the Jews doubted Jesus and the miracles. In contrast, the gentile centurion saw the miracles and had no doubt about who Jesus was. Jesus was most impressed with the faith of this non-Jew. Jesus foretells that Abraham, Isaac and Jacob will be in the New Jerusalem having dinner banquets. Many gentiles such as this centurion will join them at these banquets. These are people of the nations who live on the new earth who have lived faithful, temporal lives and are given the reward of access into the New Jerusalem. But those Jews who rejected Jesus will not have access into the New Jerusalem to sit at the feasts in the presence of the radiant glory of God, which is seven times more intense than the sun. By comparison, the light on the new earth outside the New Jerusalem will be like darkness. All the beauty of the perfect and incorruptible new creation will not compare with the indescribable experience inside the New Jerusalem at the throne of God and the Lamb. Nothing on the new earth will be adequate to satisfy the desire to be in the presence of God. Probably every human can identify with this feeling of emptiness from having sought to fulfill their inherent desire for God with something or someone, yet not finding any substitute to be adequate no matter how wonderful or marvelous the object of the pursuit is. Being in the New Jerusalem is not about prestige or prominence or elitism, but it is being in a face-to-face and heart-to-heart and soul-to-soul and spirit-to-spirit eternal intimate relationship with the godhead, whose very presence will overwhelm all the wonders of the New Jerusalem. Every human, whether Jew or gentile, who is denied access to the New Jerusalem will be eternally occupied with their lost opportunity. All the beauty of the new earth and the new heavens will not be sufficient to satisfy their longing for the personal and intimate presence of God in the New Jerusalem. As they are eternally confined to the comparative darkness of the new earth, they will weep and gnash their teeth. They will be like Esau who realized too late the wonderful inheritance he forfeited and squandered away, Hebrews 12:16–17. This is being hurt by the second death, Revelation 2:11.

It is understandable that some will think that God's merciful and gracious character is being overlooked in making these statements. As covered in the chapter "Eternal Rewards," God's forgiveness and mercy do abound to every human *while they are in this temporal life.* The time to seek the abundant mercy and grace of God is now. It is essential that believers not confuse the purpose of the High Priest at the throne of grace with the purpose of Jesus Christ at the judgment seat. Truly the Bible is full of passages about God's desire to restore wayward believers to fellowship with Him every time they come to Him in repentance. However, the judgment seat of Jesus Christ is not the place to start repenting. It will be too late. There will be many unbelievers who will repent at the great white throne judgment, but there will be no mercy shown to them. This is God's truth. There is no passage of Scripture that says there will be an opportunity for reconciliation for anyone when they stand in judgment before Jesus Christ. This is all the more true for born-again believers who live in the flesh and rebel against God after they have received His precious gift of eternal salvation. Fortunately for those defiant believers, they will be shown the mercy of not being cast into the eternal lake of fire with the unbelievers. Regarding the judgment of fleshly believers, Paul appropriately writes, "He will suffer loss; but he himself will be saved, yet so as through fire" (1 Corinthians 3:15, NASB). Paul gave a very sobering warning to the church in Galatia about the judgment of believers by Jesus Christ.

> Do not be deceived, God is not mocked; for whatever a man sows, this he will also reap. For the one who sows to his own flesh will from the flesh reap corruption, but the one who sows to the Spirit will from the Spirit reap eternal life.

> Galatians 6:7–8 (NASB)

The names of rebellious believers will be blotted out of the Lamb's book of life and they will spend eternity separated from Jesus Christ. The judicial verdicts rendered by Jesus Christ at His judgment seat will not conflict with, nor will they compromise His loving nature that motivated Him to suffer the rejection and the agony of dying on the cross to pay for the sins of the world. In reality, the unfaithful believers are the ones who overlooked, and even rejected, the the merciful and gracious character of God in their temporal lives. Therefore, these disloyal believers will spend eternity weeping and gnashing their teeth on the new earth. This is God's truth, which is in perfect alignment with His impeccable divine character.

It is also understandable that some will think these statements are in conflict with what John writes in the first part of Revelation 21.

> And I heard a loud voice from the throne, saying, "Behold, the tabernacle of God is among men, and He shall dwell among them, and they shall be His people, and God Himself shall be among them, and He shall wipe away every tear from their eyes; and there shall no longer be any death; there shall no longer be any mourning, or crying, or pain; the first things have passed away."

> Then He said to me, "It is done. I am the Alpha and the Omega, the beginning and the end. I will give to the one who thirsts from the spring of the water of life without cost. "He who overcomes will inherit these things, and I will be his God and he will be My son."

> Revelation 21:3–4 and 6–7 (NASB)

The tears, death, mourning, crying and pain that will be removed by God are all related to sufferings of this temporal physical life. Physical illness, death, and tragedy bring much mourning and sorrow in this temporal life. These are the "first things" that will not exist on the new earth because everyone will be in perfect eternal bodies that will never be become sick, or grow old, or decay, or die. There will be, however, those on the new earth who will be regretful and will weep as a result of being denied eternal rewards, because they lived in rebellion to their Savior who redeemed them with His own precious blood. Their sorrow will not be related to any hardships that happened during their temporal lives, which are the "first things" that will pass away. Instead, their sorrow will be related to their new eternal circumstance of being deprived access into the glorious presence of God and the Lamb. God will not wipe away the tears that are related to one's justly–deserved eternal circumstance. In verse 7 John adds the statement "He who overcomes will inherit these things." The inheritance includes the drinking from the water of life, which is in the New Jerusalem. Earlier in this chapter, a close examination was made of the term overcome to determine the meaning. Believers who walk away from God after salvation are not overcomers, and they risk having their names blotted out of the Lamb's books of life. Isaiah wrote a prophecy that parallels what John wrote in Revelation 21:3-4.

> The LORD of hosts will prepare a lavish banquet for all peoples on this mountain; A banquet of aged wine, choice pieces with marrow, And refined, aged wine.
> And on this mountain He will swallow up the covering which is over all peoples, Even the veil which is stretched over all nations.
> He will swallow up death for all time, And the Lord GOD will wipe tears away from all faces, And He will

remove the reproach of His people from all the earth; For the LORD has spoken.

Isaiah 25:6–8 (NASB)

Twice in this prophecy Isaiah writes that God will accomplish these things "on this mountain", meaning the eternal Mt. Zion where the New Jerusalem will be located. The literal translation from the Hebrew is worded, "The Lord of hosts made for all the peoples on this mountain a banquet." The banquet is for "all those people on this mountain" which refers to those who have access to, or who reside in the New Jerusalem. On this mountain, the Lord will also remove the covering and veil which covered the nations and people, which refers to Satan's evil kingdom of darkness that has been present on earth since the fall of Adam. These are more of the "first things" identified by John that will pass away. In addition, there will be an end to physical death and the tears and the reproach associated with this temporal life. All the sorrows from the hardships of the temporal life will be removed, but there will still be sorrow and tears for those who are not allowed to attend any of the lavish banquets the Lord will give on His eternal holy mountain.

The Creator has rightly and justly designed His created beings so that they cannot find joy in His creation either now or in eternity without first seeking and finding a real and personal relationship with the Him. Believers who continue to deny God a personal relationship after salvation will rightly be denied by God access to His amazing presence and personal relationship in the eternal estate. In contrast, those who reside on the new earth and have access into the New Jerusalem to experience God will cherish life on the wondrous new earth. Jesus spoke three prophetic parables about the kingdom of heaven in which He warns disobedient and unfaithful children about being denied access into the New Jerusalem and about being cast into the outer darkness where they will have weeping and gnashing of teeth, Matthew 11:8–13, Matthew 22:1–14 and Mathew 25:1–30. Those who are denied the wonders of the New Jerusalem will have sorrow when they hear this timeless psalm of King David.

> I was glad when they said to me, "Let us go to the house of the Lord." Our feet are standing within your gates, O Jerusalem.
>
> Psalm 122:1–2 (NASB)

The marriage supper of the Lamb was covered briefly at the beginning of this chapter. Matthew records the following parable from Jesus about the marriage supper that was in reality a warning to the Jews of that generation that they were in danger of missing out on this great occasion.

> Jesus spoke to them again in parables, saying,
> "The kingdom of heaven may be compared to a king who gave a wedding feast for his son.
> "And he sent out his slaves to call those who had been invited to the wedding feast, and they were unwilling to come.
> "Again he sent out other slaves saying, 'Tell those who have been invited, "Behold, I have prepared my dinner; my oxen and my fattened livestock are *all* butchered and everything is ready; come to the wedding feast."'
> "But they paid no attention and went their way, one to his own farm, another to his business, and the rest seized his slaves and mistreated them and killed them.
> "But the king was enraged, and he sent his armies and destroyed those murderers and set their city on fire.
> "Then he said to his slaves, 'The wedding is ready, but those who were invited were not worthy.
> "'Go therefore to the main highways, and as many as you find *there,* invite to the wedding feast.'

"Those slaves went out into the streets and gathered together all they found, both evil and good; and the wedding hall was filled with dinner guests.

"But when the king came in to look over the dinner guests, he saw a man there who was not dressed in wedding clothes, and he said to him, 'Friend, how did you come in here without wedding clothes?' And the man was speechless.

"Then the king said to the servants, 'Bind him hand and foot, and throw him into the outer darkness; in that place there will be weeping and gnashing of teeth.'

"For many are called, but few are chosen."

Matthew 22:1–14 (NASB)

The King is God the Father, and the Son is Jesus Christ. The invited guests are the people Israel. By rejecting Jesus as the Messiah, they were also rejecting the invitation to the wedding feast, which is the marriage supper of the Lamb. God punished Israel for their rejection by the conquest of the Roman army in AD 70 when their city was burned. The guests invited from the highways are the gentiles, who responded to the invitation through the ministry of Paul. In verse 11, the King noticed a man who was not dressed in wedding clothes, which refers to the white garments that are the righteous acts of the saints, Revelation 3:18 and 19:8. This is a man whose name was erased from the Lamb's Book of Life and is not allowed in the New Jerusalem. The King will have the man bound and thrown out into the outer darkness. Verse 14 is a warning to all believers. Every believer is called, but few will qualify to be the bride of the Lamb or to enter to take part in the marriage supper of the Lamb. Some would say this prophetic parable is for Israel only. However, as covered in the previous chapter, each believer's eternal status and rewards are based on works after salvation in every dispensation of human history. This prophetic parable is timeless. In Revelation 19:9,

John is told to write, "Blessed are those who are invited to the marriage supper of the Lamb" (NASB). Not every believer living on the new earth will be invited or welcome.

Knowing these things, the warnings given by the Apostle Paul are all the more real, and it is understandable that he feared being disqualified himself.

> Therefore I run in such a way, as not without aim; I box in such a way, as not beating the air; but I discipline my body and make it my slave, so that, after I have preached to others, I myself will not be disqualified.
>
> 1 Corinthians 9:26–27 (NASB)

> So then, my beloved, just as you have always obeyed, not as in my presence only, but now much more in my absence, work out your salvation with fear and trembling;
>
> Philippians 2:12 (NASB)

This chapter on the eternal city of God is seemingly and admittedly focused on the negative side of the eternal estate. It is much preferred that this chapter be about the marvelous place the new heavens and the new earth and the New Jerusalem will be. The negative has been emphasized because the majority of Christians believe the bride of Christ is solely made up of all believers of the church age, and that they will all automatically be residents of the New Jerusalem. There are many passages of Scripture that contradict this idea. This chapter is burdensome and negative to believers who want to live in the flesh. For the believers who genuinely want the best relationship possible with Jesus Christ and God the Father, the desire of this chapter is to motivate those believers to endeavor all the more to be filled with the Holy Spirit and to grow in the Word of God and to live repentant lives. The purpose of this book is not to persuade believers in the interpretation of biblical prophecy. The goal is that the prophecies inspire believers to pursue God with all their beings. The hope is that believers will aspire to be included in the role of faithful believers listed in Hebrews 11. The very purpose for which the writer of Hebrews includes the list of faithful believers of the past is to inspire believers today to obedience and vigilance.

> Therefore, since we have so great a cloud of witnesses surrounding us, let us also lay aside every encumbrance and the sin which so easily entangles us, and let us run with endurance the race that is set before us, fixing our eyes on Jesus, the author and perfecter of faith, who for the joy set before Him endured the cross, despising the shame, and has sat down at the right hand of the throne of God.
>
> Hebrews 12:1–2 (NASB)

This is a struggle, but not an impossible task for any believer. The faithful listed in Hebrews 11 were certainly not perfect sinless people. There have been those who try to persuade believers to be faithful and obedient by threatening those who fail that they have lost their salvation, or declare that they must have never been saved. These are cruel lies. Jesus Christ will rightly and justly deny many believers eternal rewards, but Jesus Christ will never ever for all eternity deny the salvation that anyone has received as a gift through faith in His death and resurrection, 2 Timothy 2:11–13. Every human who has become a child of God through faith has made a crucial decision about their eternal status and destiny, desiring to avoid the eternal lake of fire. But our planning for the eternal estate must not stop with that decision. Residence in the New Jerusalem is reserved for believers striving for a personal intimate relationship with God, the heroes of faith who are willing to sacrifice the pursuit of temporal pleasures in this life to gain the eternal pleasure of the New Jerusalem. At the other end of the spectrum are the believers who have no access to the New Jerusalem because they spent their lives after salvation in continual pursuit of pleasures of this life to feed their old-flesh natures. A one-time decision of faith changed our eternal destiny: we are no longer bound for the lake of fire, but we are now children of God. But as children of God there are continuous decisions we must make day by day about the status we desire in the eternal estate. Is being excluded from the gathering to Jesus Christ from the earth to be His eternal bride acceptable to me? Do I care that all my works will be burned up and my name will be erased from the Lamb's book of life as everyone watches at the judgment seat of Jesus Christ? Is it all right that I will just stay at my home on the new earth while many people I know go to experience the marvelous wonder of the New Jerusalem? Will I be fine when they return glowing with the radiant glory of God, trying to describe the indescribable pleasures of being at the throne of God and the Lamb, eating the fruit of the tree, and drinking from the spring of the water of life? Are the pursuits of the fleeting wanton pleasures of this temporal life so wonderful that they are worth forfeiting the eternal pleasures of the abundant eternal life? Will this be a good tradeoff? Should I be running to the throne of grace of my High Priest seeking His help in my time of weakness and need? Should I be using the mighty power of the Holy Spirit God made to dwell in me to put my old-flesh nature to death?

> For if you are living according to the flesh, you must die; but if by the Spirit you are putting to death the deeds of the body, you will live.
>
> Romans 8:13 (NASB)

The phrase "you will live" is referring to the abundant eternal life. In reality, putting the flesh nature to death daily by the Holy Spirit is not a burden, but it is the lifting of a great burden from us. When we are walking by faith, the Holy Spirit enables us to obey, therefore the commandments of God are not burdensome.

> For this is the love of God, that we keep His commandments; and His commandments are not burdensome.
>
> 1 John 5:3 (NASB)

The struggle is to stay walking in the power of the Holy Spirit. Living our temporal lives so as to gain the abundant eternal life requires sacrificing the pursuit of the things for which the flesh nature lusts. It seems like a costly sacrifice now, but when standing in the New Jerusalem, the sacrifice will become minuscule in comparison to the eternal blessings. In reality, all it costs any believer is a closer and more intimate walk with Jesus Christ now by the power of His Holy Spirit. That cost is no burden at all, but is a great and wonderful blessing. I exhort every believer, don't risk missing out on the unique and awesome blessing of being the bride of Christ, of gaining entrance into the New Jerusalem, and many other unfathomable riches Jesus desires to give out as eternal rewards. Even the Apostle Paul had to be diligent to make sure that he was not excluded from the rewards.

> And everyone who competes in the games exercises self-control in all things. They then do it to receive a perishable wreath, but we an imperishable. Therefore I run in such a way, as not without aim; I box in such a way, as not beating the air; but I buffet my body and make it my slave, lest possibly, after I have preached to others, I myself should be disqualified.
>
> 1 Corinthians 9:25–27 (NASB)

For as long as Paul was alive in this temporal life, he remained vigilant in the battle to be included with those who overcome and prevail.

I have fought the good fight, I have finished the course, I have kept the faith; in the future there is laid up for me the crown of righteousness, which the Lord, the righteous Judge, will award to me on that day; and not only to me, but also to all who have loved His appearing.

2 Timothy 4:7–8 (NASB)

Christians who walk in disobedience give little or no thought to the coming of Jesus Christ. Only the true bride is ready, looks forward to, and loves the appearing of the Bridegroom.

He who testifies to these things says, "Surely I am coming quickly." Amen. Even so, come, Lord Jesus.

Revelation 22:20 (KJV)

A PRAYER FOR THE ETERNAL

I pray, Heavenly Father, that you enable me, the finite, to be ever focused on Your awesome, infinite, eternal, omnipotent being; that I the finite be continually obedient to You; that I the finite be continually humble before You and living in the reality that my being is completely and totally dependent on You; and that nothing is ever going to change that, but it doesn't need to change, for there is nothing in error or flawed in Your plan for my existence. There is nothing that can be done to improve Your plan for my existence, that You have brought me into existence without my even having awareness of my existence nor Your existence. You brought me forth in a state of sin, fallen, separated from You so that I can know from the beginning of my existence the sorrow, the pain, the misery, the suffering, the agony, the tragedy of being in existence yet separated from You. You have revealed Yourself to me, and you revealed myself to me and offered me by Your grace a wondrous eternal destiny with You through Your Beloved eternal Son, Jesus Christ my Savior. You have given me the option of pursuing that destiny or pursuing a destiny apart from You, denying You, depriving You, hating you, loathing You, rejecting You, abandoning You—thinking I can do all and be all that I desire to be apart from You, thinking that my will for me is better than Your will for me, a fool's errand, an effort of futility, the pursuit of death, destruction, and misery. Heavenly Father, I choose to pursue light and life and truth, to pursue You, the One out of whom my existence is. I pray, Heavenly Father, that You will enable me to live my life so that I will be found worthy by You to have an eternal dwelling place in Your eternal holy house and never have need to leave Your eternal holy house again, that I be a pillar in Your eternal holy house with the name of Your eternal holy city written upon me, and Your name written upon me, and the new name of Your eternal beloved Son written upon me. I pray, my Lord and Savior Jesus, Son of God, You who are the King of kings and Lord of lords, You who are the Alpha and Omega, the beginning and the end, the first and the last, the first born of the creation, You who are the Lamb of God slain before the foundation of the world, You who are the resurrection and the life, You who have created all by the word of Your power and uphold all things by the word of Your power, You who are the bread who has come down out of heaven, You who are the light that has come forth into darkness, You who are the way, the truth and the life, You who are the Bridegroom, You who are the Bright and Moring Star, You who are the Good Shepherd who laid down His life for the sheep, You who are the door whereby the sheep may enter and go in and out and find pasture, You who have made purification for sin and are seated at the right hand of the Father awaiting Your Father to make Your enemies to be a footstool for Your feet. I pray my Lord that You will enable me to live my life so that as You are preparing dwelling places in Your Father's eternal holy house, that You will find me worthy to prepare a place there for me also, and when You come again to receive Your kingdom of priests, Your holy nation, Your eternal bride unto Yourself, that you will receive me also along with them, that I will thus be with You forever and never be separated from you again for all eternity, and that you proclaim my name to Your Father in Your Father's eternal holy house, that I be eternally one with You and with Your Father by the power of Your Holy Spirit in Your Father's eternal holy house forever and ever. Amen.